Student Handbook to Psychology

Methods
and Measurements

Volume II

Student Handbook to Psychology

Methods
and Measurements

Volume II

BERNARD C. BEINS

An Infobase Learning Company

Student Handbook to Psychology: Methods and Measurements
Copyright © 2012 Bernard C. Beins

Facts On File, Inc.
An Imprint of Infobase Learning
132 West 31st Street
New York NY 10001

Library of Congress Cataloging-in-Publication Data
Student handbook to psychology / [edited by] Bernard C. Beins.
     v. ; cm.
  Includes bibliographical references and index.
  Contents: v. 1. History, perspectives, and applications / Kenneth D. Keith—v. 2. Methods and measurements / Bernard C. Beins—v. 3. Brain and mind / Michael Kerchner—v. 4. Learning and thinking / Christopher M. Hakala and Bernard C. Beins—v. 5. Developmental psychology / Lynn Shelley—v. 6. Personality and abnormal psychology / Janet F. Carlson—v. 7. Social psychology / Jeffrey D. Holmes and Sheila K. Singh.
  ISBN 978-0-8160-8280-3 (set : alk. paper)—ISBN 978-0-8160-8281-0 (v. 1 : alk. paper)—ISBN 978-0-8160-8286-5 (v. 2 : alk. paper)—ISBN 978-0-8160-8285-8 (v. 3 : alk. paper)—ISBN 978-0-8160-8284-1 (v. 4 : alk. paper)—ISBN 978-0-8160-8282-7 (v. 5 : alk. paper)—ISBN 978-0-8160-8287-2 (v. 6 : alk. paper)—ISBN 978-0-8160-8283-4 (v. 7 : alk. paper) 1. Psychology—Textbooks. I. Beins, Bernard.
  BF121.S884 2012
  150—dc23   2011045277

Facts On File books are available at special discounts when purchased in bulk quantities for businesses, associations, institutions, or sales promotions. Please call our Special Sales Department in New York at (212) 967-8800 or (800) 322-8755.

You can find Facts On File on the World Wide Web at http://www.infobaselearning.com

Excerpts included herewith have been reprinted by permission of the copyright holders; author has made every effort to contact copyright holders. The publishers will be glad to rectify, in future editions, any errors or omissions brought to their notice.

Text design by Erika K. Arroyo
Cover design by Takeshi Takahashi
Composition by EJB Publishing Services
Cover printed by Yurchak Printing, Landisville, Pa.
Book printed and bound by Yurchak Printing, Landisville, Pa.
Date printed: September 2012
Printed in the United States of America

This book is printed on acid-free paper.

CONTENTS

PREFACE

Behavior is endlessly fascinating. People and other animals are complicated creatures that show extraordinary patterns of abilities, intelligence, social interaction, and creativity along with, unfortunately, problematic behaviors. All of these characteristics emerge because of the way the brain interprets incoming information and directs our responses to that information.

This seven-volume **Student Handbook to Psychology** set highlights important and interesting facets of thought and behavior. It provides a solid foundation for learning about psychological processes associated with growth and development, social issues, thinking and problem solving, and abnormal thought and behavior. Most of the major schools and theories related to psychology appear in the books in the series, albeit in abbreviated form. Because psychology is such a highly complex and diverse discipline, these volumes present a broad overview of the subject rather than a complete and definitive treatise. Such a work, in fact, would be difficult (if not impossible) because psychological scientists are still searching for answers to a great number of questions. If you are interested in delving in more depth into specific areas of psychology, we have provided a bibliography of accessible readings to help you fill in the details.

The volumes in this series follow the order that you might see in a standard presentation on a variety of topics, but each book stands alone and the series does not need to be read in any particular order. In fact, you can peruse individual chapters in each volume at will, seeking out and focusing on those topics that interest you most. On the other hand, if you do choose to read through a complete volume, you will find a flow of information that connects related sections of the books, providing a coherent overview of the entire discipline of psychology.

The authors of the seven volumes in this series are experts in their respective fields, so you will find psychological concepts that are up to date and that reflect the most recent advances in scientific knowledge about thought and behavior. In addition, each of the authors is an excellent writer who has presented the information in an interesting and compelling fashion. Although some of the material and many of the ideas are complex, the authors have done an outstanding job of conveying those ideas in ways that are both interesting and effective.

In *History, Perspectives, and Applications*, Professor Kenneth Keith of the University of San Diego has woven historical details into a tapestry that shows how psychological questions originated within a philosophical framework, incorporated biological concepts, and ultimately evolved into a single scientific discipline that remains interconnected with many other academic and scientific disciplines. Dr. Keith has identified the major figures associated with the development of the field of psychology as well as the social forces that helped shape their ideas.

In *Methods and Measurements*, I illustrate how psychologists create new knowledge through research. The volume presents the major approaches to research and explains how psychologists develop approaches to research that help us answer questions about complex aspects of behavior. Without these well-structured and proven research methods, we would not have much of the information we now have about behavior. Furthermore, these methods, approaches, and practices provide confidence that the knowledge we do have is good knowledge, grounded in solid research.

Many people are under the impression that each thought or behavior is a single thing. In *Brain and Mind*, Professor Michael Kerchner of Washington College dispels this impression by showing how the myriad structures and functions of our brain work in unison to create those seemingly simple and one-dimensional behaviors. As the author explains, each behavior is really the result of many different parts of the brain engaging in effective communication with one another. Professor Kerchner also explains what occurs when this integration breaks down.

Learning and Thinking, co-authored by Professor Christopher Hakala of Western New England College and me (at Ithaca College), explores the fascinating field of cognitive psychology, a discipline focused on the processes by which people learn, solve problems, and display intelligence. Cognitive psychology is a fascinating field that explores how we absorb information, integrate it, and then act on it.

In *Developmental Psychology*, Professor Lynn Shelley of Westfield State University addresses the very broad area of psychology that examines how people develop and change from the moment of conception through old age. Dr. Shelley's detailed and compelling explanation includes a focus on how maturation and environment play a part in shaping how each individual grows, evolves, and changes.

In *Personality and Abnormal Psychology*, Professor Janet Carlson of the Buros Center for Testing at the University of Nebraska (Lincoln) addresses various dimensions of personality, highlighting processes that influence normal and abnormal facets of personality. Dr. Carlson also explains how psychologists study the fundamental nature of personality and how it unfolds.

The final volume in this series is *Social Psychology*. Co-authored by Professor Jeffrey Holmes of Ithaca College and Sheila Singh of Cornell University, this volume examines how our thoughts and behaviors emerge in connection with our interactions with other people. As the authors of this volume explain, changes in a person's social environment can lead to notable changes in the way that person thinks and behaves.

As editor of this series, I have had the opportunity to work with all of the authors who have contributed their expertise and insights to this project. During this collaborative process, I found that we have much in common. All of us have spent our careers pondering why people think and act the way they do. For every answer we come up with, we also develop new questions that are just as interesting and important. And we all agree that you cannot find a more interesting subject to study than psychology.

As you learn about psychology, we hope that the information in these seven volumes inspires the same fascination in you. We also hope that our explanations, illustrations, and narrative studies motivate you to continue studying why we humans are the way we are.

—Bernard C. Beins, Ph.D., Professor of Psychology,
Ithaca College, Series Editor

CHAPTER 1

THE NATURE OF PSYCHOLOGICAL RESEARCH

Psychology is an empirical science. This means that psychologists base their knowledge about how people think and act on the results of scientific research. The number of domains of everyday life that involve psychological research is extensive, and it continues to grow. Very often, people see the results of psychological research applied to their lives without knowing about the research that led to those results.

For example, if a clinical psychologist wants to treat a client effectively, that psychologist needs to know what therapeutic approach works best. The only way to determine effectiveness is by conducting research studies. If educators want to know what approaches to teaching and learning will be most effective in schools, they need to carry out research that allows them to differentiate between strategies that work and those that do not.

Regarding the use of new technologies, if legislators want to know whether they should ban the use of cell phones while people drive, psychologists can conduct research to see the extent to which driving performance deteriorates if people talk or send text messages on a cell phone while driving.

Psychologists conduct this kind of research for a variety of reasons. Sometimes researchers engage in a project because they have a practical question to answer. For example, which approach will provide the most effective treatments for psychological disorders. In other cases, researchers want to test theories. There are even times that psychologists observe something and simply wonder why people act as they do. An illustration of this involved a woman named Kitty

Genovese who was attacked and murdered. It was initially believed that no witnesses helped her, and this belief led psychologists to create some very ingenious experiments to find out when people will help somebody in need and when they are likely not to help.

Psychologists regularly study behavior in the lab rather than in the everyday world. Very often there is a trade-off between the complexity of a research setting and the degree of control that the researcher has over a given situation. If the psychologist conducts the research in a complex, real world environment, there is a great likelihood that many things going on in that environment may influence the behavior of people or animals being studied. An additional complication is that it is hard to know which of these things are really affecting subjects' behavior.

On the other hand, to simplify things, the researcher could conduct a study in the laboratory. This setting removes many forces that could affect behavior, so the researcher can concentrate on one or two factors. The simplicity allows the researcher to draw more certain conclusions. But by moving the research to a lab, the psychologist is also making the setting somewhat artificial, and this raises the question of whether the simple laboratory experience resembles what people normally do. That is, does the behavior of people in a laboratory resemble what they would do in everyday life? In the case of providing help, getting involved in a situation in which somebody is being murdered is not likely to be the same as getting involved in helping somebody in a laboratory.

One issue related to generalizing from the lab to the real world involves research with animals. Most psychologists study human behavior, but since the early days of psychology in the United States, researchers have also studied animal behavior. For example, John Watson, who is generally recognized as the father of behaviorism, studied learning in rats. And B.F. Skinner, who was probably the most famous psychologist of the 1960s, conducted much of his research with pigeons. Other psychologists have studied behavior in animals as diverse as chimpanzees, monkeys, dogs, cats, mice, cockroaches, and even mealworms.

What purpose is there for studying such animals? There are two general answers to this question. First, it is interesting to understand the behavior of animals in its own right. At times, such research can have practical applications. For example, investigators have studied the normal behavior of domesticated farm animals so they can identify behaviors that are abnormal and, by extension, identify the reasons or causes for the abnormalities (such as abnormal behavior that might be caused by overcrowding).

A second reason for studying nonhuman animals is that the results of such research can help people. Noted psychologist Neal Miller pointed out that researchers have relied on animal research to study a variety of issues relevant to people, like anorexia, stress, responses to pain, and depression.

Sometimes the behavioral and biological activity of mice can help us understand people. *(Wikipedia)*

Recent research has shown that the brains of mice can produce a substance that, when present, prevents depression-like symptoms like social withdrawal. Experiments with the mice show that a particular part of the brain called the nucleus accumbens, a reward center in the brain, is particularly affected by this substance. Autopsies on the brains of people who had been depressed have revealed a deficiency in this substance, suggesting that the same processes affecting depression are at work both in mice and in people. The obvious corollary here is that finding a treatment for mice may also lead to more effective treatments for people. Naturally, mice brains are not identical to human brains, so work with mice will not lead to all the answers to questions about the occurrence and treatment of depression, but it may point in the right direction.

In addition to using animals to study biological processes that take place in humans, psychologists also use animals like rats and mice to study human behavior. A fundamental issue related to such research is whether a rodent's behavior really resembles human behavior. Clearly, humans can do things that rats cannot do, such as talk. But research on animal learning has led to well-established principles that also apply to people. For example, children with autism are often treated successfully using reinforcement principles that were initially established with animals. Reinforcement will not cure autism, but by using it, the behavior of autistic children can gradually be shaped so they can be integrated into broader social situations. Another example comes from an earlier era: Prior to the development of medications to treat people with psychiatric problems, some psychiatric institutions used programs based on reinforcement principles to change the behavior of patients.

Research on people and on animals is very difficult because both are complicated and because human and animal behavior is determined by a great number of factors. Thus, any single study will be conducted in a simpler environment than the real-life settings in which behavior occurs, so any single study can provide only a partial answer to a question about behaviors. So psychologists complete many studies—there are a lot of pieces to the puzzle, each study is one small piece.

THE GOALS OF PSYCHOLOGICAL RESEARCH

Scientific research in psychology generally moves toward one of four goals, each one increasingly more complex and difficult to reach. The first goal, which is the simplest even though it is not all that simple, is **description** of behavior. Research that achieves this goal documents the presence of a behavior of interest in a given situation. One well known pattern of behavior that psychologists have described has to do with learning information or a new skill. Research has shown that it is better to study or to practice in multiple, small sessions rather than in a single, long session. So even if two people spend the same amount of time studying, the one who studies in several short sessions is likely to remember more than the one trying to learn everything in one sitting. Researchers have observed and described this phenomenon over and over. It has become an established principle in psychology, and it meets the most elementary goal of research.

Sometimes scientists want to go beyond simple description, however. Sometimes the goal is **prediction** about when a behavior will occur or what the behavior will be. Making this kind of prediction presupposes that the psychologist already knows something about the behavior in the first place. That is, the behavior needs to have been described already so that the psychologist knows it actually exists. Otherwise, the researcher wastes time trying to generate a behavior that is not likely to occur at all.

Researchers have conducted many studies on helping behavior (i.e., when people help others and when they choose not to). One consideration is the degree to which a person identifies with the person needing help. The greater the identification, the more likely the potential helper is to offer assistance. So a reasonable prediction would be that people would be more inclined to offer help if they are asked to increase their empathy for a person needing help. In fact, research has supported this prediction.

The third level of knowledge in research is **explanation** of why a behavior happens as it does. Once psychologists have described a behavior and predicted its occurrence, the next goal is to figure out why it happens. Explanations are difficult because most behavior is not the result of a single cause; there are always multiple factors at work.

For example, researchers are attempting to find the causes of autism. In the past, one now-discredited explanation was that mothers of autistic children were emotionally cold and withdrawn from their children, which caused the type of withdrawal that autistic children often show. The term used to describe these mothers was *refrigerator mothers*. Many psychologists and psychiatrists accepted this explanation for several decades. A subsequent proposal was that autism was caused by thimerosal, a chemical preservative used in childhood vaccines. Although research has shown that thimerosal is not implicated in autism, some people still maintain a belief in this explanation. Most recently, investigators have begun to develop genetic explanations for autism.

It is easy to describe autistic behavior but much harder to predict whether symptoms will appear. Because autism's heritability is high, there is some familial predictability. As of now, however, scientists still do not have a complete explanation for autism or who is likely to be afflicted by autism.

It is generally true that the more complex or controversial a behavior, the more likely that there will be competing attempts at explanation. Over the long term, research can help psychologists develop greater confidence in some explanations and discard those that research does not support.

The final goal of research is **control**. If psychologists have described a behavior, learned to predict when it will occur, and generated an explanation for it, they may also be able to control it. For example, suppose a child is disruptive in the classroom. We can predict that the disruptions will continue if the behaviors are reinforced or rewarded. The explanation, according to behavioral theory, is that reinforcement will exacerbate the behavior. Not providing reinforcement should lead to extinction of the behavior. Thus, a useful strategy for controlling the disruptive child's behavior can simply be to ignore the child. If misbehaving is not reinforced, the unwanted behavior should disappear. In other words, the behavior can be controlled. Although

(continues on page 8)

The Mozart Effect: Does Music Make You Smarter?

A research team conducted an experiment to determine whether listening to music could improve people's performance in a problem-solving task. The work was based on previous research showing that musically oriented children showed better spatial skills than nonmusical children did.

So the researchers created groups that listened to music composed by Wolfgang Amadeus Mozart or engaged in a relaxation exercise or sat in silence. After participation in one of the three study conditions, each of the subjects took a test. Based on the resulting data, the researchers estimated the participants' spatial IQ scores and found that participants who listened to Mozart's music scored the highest.

Subsequently, a different research team investigated whether the Mozart effect could be replicated. They also created three groups—one that listened to Mozart, one that listened to music by composer Philip Glass, and one that

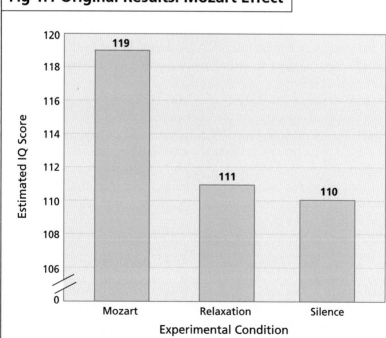

Fig 1.1 Original Results: Mozart Effect

Source: Rauscher, Frances H., Gordon L. Shaw, and Katherine N. Ky. "Listening to Mozart enhances spatial-temporal reasoning: towards a neurophysiological basis." *Neuroscience Letters* 185 (1995): 44–47.

© Infobase Learning

sat in silence. They found only small, unreliable differences in the scores for participants, results that indicated an insignificant correlation between IQ and the three conditions used in their study. Other research also failed to replicate the original results.

The case of the Mozart effect illustrates how science is supposed to work. The measurements (test scores) were objective. The conclusions were data driven; that is, they were based on data rather than on opinion or intuition. The procedure was replicable; the researchers who created the initial study provided enough information so that other researchers could test their results. Finally, the study was published in a scientific journal, thus making it public.

So even though the Mozart effect does not appear to be real, the scientific process worked well. Researchers proposed and tested an idea in a way that others could follow up on their findings, and ultimately, psychologists were able to draw a conclusion in which they had confidence.

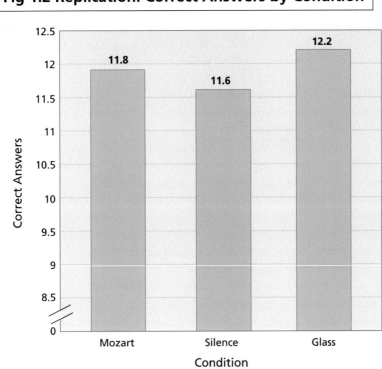

Fig 1.2 Replication: Correct Answers by Condition

Source: Steele, Kenneth M., Karen E. Bass, and Melissa D. Crook. "The mystery of the Mozart effect: failure to replicate." *Psychological Science* 10, no. 4 (July 1999): 366–369.

© Infobase Learning

(continued from page 5)

psychologists have shown this approach to be effective, this strategy will not always work, not because it is flawed but simply because there are generally multiple causes for behavior.

WHAT CONSTITUTES SCIENTIFIC KNOWLEDGE?

The knowledge that psychologists develop in their research is scientific. This is different from the knowledge that people develop in everyday life. Scientific knowledge is developed through systematic programs of research in which new knowledge builds on old. There are four main characteristics of scientific knowledge.

First, scientific knowledge is **objective**. This means that scientists define their terms so that there is no ambiguity about what they are discussing. For example, when studying intelligence, researchers often use a score on a test as a clearly defined measurement of intelligence. This approach ensures that everybody knows what *intelligence* means in the context of the research; no matter who does the testing, the intelligence score is clearly defined. In everyday life, people are generally more subjective in defining intelligence, so two people may or may not agree how intelligent a given individual might be.

A second characteristic of scientific knowledge is that it is **data driven,** which means that scientists base their conclusions on data from research. If the results of research do not support initial beliefs, the researchers may change their beliefs based on the research-derived data.

A further aspect of scientific knowledge is that it needs to be developed so other researchers can evaluate it further. That is, it has to be **verifiable**. Psychologists plan their studies very carefully to ensure confidence in their results. But sometimes things go wrong because of things beyond a researcher's control; in some cases, the researcher has no way of knowing about these things and is thus unaware that anything is wrong. For example, some of the people in a study might have been having a bad day, so they behave in unusual ways. Or they might have been an atypical group, so their behavior might not be like that of most other people. And sometimes, there are hidden flaws in the design of the study that the researchers failed to see.

Other researchers can **replicate** a study to see if they get the same results. If the same results occur, psychologists gain confidence in the conclusions. If the results are different, it means that further research is needed because it is not clear which of the studies yielded more valid results.

The final characteristic of scientific knowledge is that it is **public**. In other words, it is important that researchers make the details of their studies available for others to evaluate. If the scientists keep such information secret, others are not able to evaluate how well the research was done, whether the conclusions follow logically from the data, or if repeating the study will lead to the same results. Generally, researchers make their work available to others by publishing it in scientific journals or by presenting it at professional conferences.

DIFFERENT TYPES OF RESEARCH

Psychology is a broad-based discipline with research that shares elements with many other domains, like sociology, anthropology, linguistics, biology, and others. Consequently, psychologists borrow research methodologies freely from other disciplines. In addition, in some psychological studies, the investigators can exert great control over the research environment, whereas in other studies, the investigators might want to see how behaviors occur in more complex, natural environments.

Because of the diversity of approaches to research, psychologists have adopted many different research techniques, each of which has its own strengths and weaknesses. In situations where psychologists can control an environment extensively, they prefer an experimental approach that is characterized by manipulating variables systematically. On the other hand, if conducting research in a natural setting that they cannot control, psychologists may simply let behaviors unfold as they normally do, recording those behaviors that occur.

In cases in which researchers want to collect a lot of detailed information, they might use surveys and questionnaires to find out what a large number of people think, case studies to investigate a single person, or longitudinal research that spans a long period of time. Psychologists have used a lot of creativity and ingenuity in developing techniques for answering complex questions about behavior.

The research approaches listed below include experiments, correlational research, observational research, survey research, longitudinal research, and archival research. These are commonly used categories for discussing research, but sometimes they overlap. The various approaches will be discussed in greater detail in later chapters.

In psychology, the term **experiment** has a specific meaning. An experiment involves research in which the investigator systematically changes a situation to see how each change affects the ways that people or other animals behave. The emphasis in this approach is on controlling the research environment so that the researcher is confident that any changes in behavior are due to the changes that the experimenter creates.

> **Correlational research** involves searching for patterns of behavior without an attempt by the investigator to manipulate the environment. This approach is useful when a researcher wants to see how

behaviors naturally unfold in a complex environment. In some cases, it is not possible for a researcher to control the situation experimentally, so correlational research is the only realistic way to conduct a study.

Observational research is descriptive research in which the psychologist identifies behaviors of interest and monitors those behaviors in a naturalistic setting. As a rule, there is no attempt to manipulate the environment. Instead, the researcher records when or how frequently and for how long behaviors occur.

Survey research involves the administration of questionnaires to a large number of people. It allows the psychologist to get a great deal of information from many people very quickly. The most frequent approach to surveys is through telephone interviews.

Longitudinal research takes place over an extended period. As a result, the researcher can see how changes occur over the course of time. Longitudinal research might last for a few weeks or months, or it can extend over years or decades, depending on the nature of the questions that the investigator is asking.

Case studies involve in-depth study of one or two people, often over a period of time. This approach permits the researcher to collect a great deal of rich information from the person or persons being studied. This technique is useful for documenting a phenomenon about which little might be known and for generating hypotheses for later research projects. It is also a useful way to study rare phenomena and behaviors.

Archival research involves using existing information or data to answer some behavioral question. Researchers using this approach rely on such materials as government records, newspapers stories, television programs, and similar sources. This way of collecting data is useful when a researcher cannot get information directly from people who, in other circumstances, might have been able to provide information in person.

CULTURAL ISSUES IN RESEARCH

People differ in many ways, including the ways they behave. There are many causes for these differences, but one reason that psychologists have studied is cultural background. Your culture influences not only the way you behave but also the way you think. Psychologists have spent a lot of time trying to determine which aspects of behavior and thought are due to culture and which aspects are nearly universal and unaffected by a person's culture. This turns out to be a very difficult task that has led to some very interesting questions.

Can You Feel the Flavor of Food?

Some rare people perceive the world differently from the rest of us. For example, one case study involved a man who explained that chicken that did not have "enough points" was not done. He experienced different shapes when he ate. Chicken that was cooked enough had points, but chicken that needed more cooking time was round. Another response was by a woman who, when she heard a particular sound, saw "blinding red jaggers." Such experiences describe **synesthesia**, a condition in which there is a mixing of sense modalities. People feel flavors or see colors and shapes or mix other senses when they hear particular sounds.

This type of response does not represent any kind of disease or mental disturbance. It is simply a different way of reacting to stimuli. It is quite rare, although nobody really knows how rare it actually is. In some cases, people are reluctant to admit to such experiences because others regard them (and the people who experience them) to be quite bizarre.

Such people are so rare that they can usually only be part of a case study. There are not enough of them to assign to different treatment groups and study experimentally. As a result, psychologists can learn a great deal about a single person, but the cause of the sensory responses remains unknown. Moreover, it is not clear whether synesthesia in different people arises from the same cause. One example of a case study that led to single-subject experiments involved the man who felt cooked chicken as pointed. A doctor named Richard Cytowic documented the case in his book *The Man Who Tasted Shapes: A Bizarre Medical Mystery Offers Revolutionary Insights into Emotions, Reasoning, and Consciousness.*

Are Psychological Concepts Universal Across Cultures?

Social and behavioral scientists call research findings that seem to be universal **etics**. Thus, etic conclusions are those that seem to be culturally neutral. That is, it is possible to discuss them without regard to any specific culture, and what would be true for one culture would hold true for all. On the other hand, when the culture of an individual affects research findings, those results are called **emics**. Psychologists have come up with some etic accounts to explain research results, but it is often the case that when the research receives further scrutiny, culture may have relevance.

One example of etic findings has to do with recognition of facial emotions. Psychologist Paul Ekman has studied people's abilities to identify specific emotions from photographs. People seem to recognize some emotions very reliably, regardless of their culture. Ekman has concluded that universal emotions include anger, disgust, fear, happiness, sadness, and surprise. So most psychologists believe that recognition of emotion has universal underpinnings and that this type of research represent etics.

On the other hand, there are cultural aspects to some expressions of emotion. People in different cultures learn to display a given emotion differently. Furthermore, there are differences in accuracy of recognition of facial emotions across cultures. For example, people are likely to recognize an emotion like disgust in others, regardless of whether they are looking at people from their own culture or from another culture. However, recognition accuracy for disgust is greater when people are looking at others within their own culture than at people of a different culture. So some aspects of the recognition of emotion may involve emics. There is a greater discrepancy across cultures for recognition of some emotions, like disgust, than for happiness.

Another area that psychologists regard as etical involves the nature of attachment between a child and a parent. Developmental psychologists identify attachment styles as secure, anxious, or ambivalent. In a research paradigm in which a caregiver (often the mother) leaves a child alone in a room and then returns, the child may (a) be happy to see the mother and wants contact with her, reflecting secure attachment, (b) avoid the mother, reflecting anxious attachment, or c) show signs of wanting contact with mother while simultaneously showing resentment, reflecting ambivalent attachment.

Research has shown that securely attached children show better social adjustment than other children do. However, most of the research on this subject has taken place with children from Western societies. What is considered "better" in terms of social adjustment in the West may differ markedly from that in other cultures. So although the research on attachment styles has led to what appear to be etics, emics are also involved.

These kinds of cultural differences take on special meaning in research on mental health issues. Sometimes the nature of questions is an important issue. For example, the **Dissociative Experiences Scale** assesses whether people integrate their thoughts, memories, and emotions in their lives. This scale can help a psychologist disgnosis psychological problems like multiple personality disorder. However, cultural differences across individuals can be of some concern. For example, one question on this scale inquires about driving a car and not remembering details of what happened during the trip. This kind of question makes sense only for groups that regularly drive; in groups that rely on public transportation or that do not use automobiles, the question would not be particularly helpful.

In addition, translating items or concepts into different languages can be problematic. One psychological test has an question that refers to a person being able to "shake off the blues." Speakers of English will recognize that "feeling blue" means feeling sad or depressed. But it is not clear how to translate that phrase into other languages. For example, using the Spanish word *azul* would not work because it does not have the same emotional meaning in Spanish that *blue* does in English.

Further complicating the discussion of etics and emics is the fact that two types of behaviors that may appear to be related may have different etic and emic status. For example, in studying eating disorders, psychologists have discovered that anorexia nervosa, an inability or unwillingness to eat, seems to be culturally invariant; that is, it has the same manifestations across cultures. On the other hand, bulimia nervosa, excessive eating followed by a compensating behavior (e.g., vomiting, fasting, using laxatives) appears to be a very Western syndrome and is far from universal.

Defining Culture, Race, and Ethnicity
Culture and ethnicity are difficult concepts to study because there are numerous pitfalls that researchers have to avoid. In spite of such problems, psychologists have learned a lot about the commonalities and differences among people in varied groups.

People may be able to recognize when others come from another culture by virtue of differences in language, attire, or food preferences. But these are only outward signs of cultural differences and do not define what culture is. Although some psychologists deal with culture by examining these external signs, others consider culture to be an internal or cognitive concept. That is, with what group does a person identify in a given situation? In this view, culture is a response, not something that exists on its own.

Because of the difficulty in even defining concepts like culture, ethnicity, and race, doing research on these issues is complex, and drawing conclusions based on the research requires caution. One implication of this complexity is that, although psychologists have asked (and answered) a lot of research questions on the relation between behavior and culture, ethnicity, and race, they still face many unanswered questions.

Regarding race, some researchers have concluded that people of various races may respond differently because of their respective race; that is, race is a causal factor. Other researchers argue that race is not a real category at all, much less a causal factor. For instance, if a person has one black parent and one white parent, to which race does that person belong? That question has an answer, but it is a socially defined answer, not a scientific answer. In the United States, a person who has any black ancestors may regard himself or herself as black, and others are quite likely to do the same. But this classification has more to do with a person's ethnic affiliation than with race per se.

One of the first issues that investigators contend with is deciding on cultural or ethnic or racial categories. This description process can be controversial because there are marked disagreements on what the categories are and who is included in each one. For example, in the United States, the Census Bureau does not include "Hispanic" as a racial category, whereas agencies dealing with civil rights do.

Adding to the complexity is the fact that the means for determining a person's race or ethnicity has changed over time. For example, across the decades, the U.S. Census Bureau determined people's race by the language they spoke, then by their last name, then by the place they were born, and now through self-report. Unfortunately, in many studies, researchers rely on governmentally determined categories that are not scientifically based and that are subject to change.

Currently, most research involving people of different cultures relies on self-identification. That is, a person is seen to belong to whatever group he or she claims to belong. A complicating issue here is that when people identify their ethnicity, they may choose different categories depending on what they are being asked to do (forced-choice questions versus selection of all categories that apply) and what the implications of their choice might be. If members of a particular group might be eligible for some tangible benefit, it makes sense for them to indicate that they are members of that group. But they may not feel an affiliation for that group as they go through their daily routines. In addition, some categories may not be at all useful. If researchers generate a category called "Asian", it will provide no useful information because there are so many different Asian cultures that a single category does not say anything about the culture with which respondents affiliate.

Finally, cultural researchers now recognize that people can belong to different cultures at the same time. Research has revealed that people in some groups that immigrate to the United States may change their behaviors within a generation or two of being in the country, but their attitudes may change very little. So the culture in which they should be categorized depends on what aspect of their life a researcher is investigating.

Cultural Differences in Psychological Research

It is easy to imagine that culture influences the things people think about but that thought processes are reasonably similar regardless of culture. However, some research suggests that people's thought processes themselves do differ across cultures in interesting ways. Those differences show how difficult it is to make general statements about psychological processes.

Studies of people who are bilingual, that is, who speak two languages, are illustrative. Recognition of facial emotions has elements that appear universal and are not affected by culture, but we cannot dismiss the effect of culture entirely. In different studies, people who were bilingual in English and either Hindi or Spanish were asked to identify emotions being expressed in photographs. They were much more accurate when the experimental session took place in English rather than when it took place either in Hindi or in Spanish. Language made a significant difference in the participants' performance, possibly because speakers of English are generally more willing to discuss emotions openly than are speakers of some other languages. Thus, a supposedly universal ability does seem to have learned, cultural components.

Similarly, when bilingual individuals who spoke English and Russian tried to retrieve memories of events in their lives, the language in which researchers tested them made a difference. When tested in Russian, people were better at remembering events that took place in a Russian context; when tested in English, they were better at remembering events in an American context. The memories of both contexts existed for these people, but language made a difference in the ease with which people could recall them. When switching from one linguistic framework to another, people may change their cognitive frameworks.

Even at the neurological level, culture seems to have an impact. Researchers have found that there are differences in brain functioning during a given task for people from different cultures. So it seems clear that culture exerts effects on psychological processes at multiple levels. As a result, understanding the psychological makeup of people requires knowledge of their culture(s) as well as of details of the context in which they are functioning at any given time.

CONCLUSION

Psychologists ask a variety of questions about thought, attitude, and behavior. The research involves issues associated with mental health that many people associate with psychology, but also with normal issues of everyday life. Psychologists study how people feel about various topics, how their personalities relate to their approaches to life, how the design of machines relates to people's ability to use those machines, and much more.

The general goals of research consist of describing psychological phenomena, predicting when they will occur, explaining why they occur, and exerting control over them. It can be fairly easy to describe behaviors accurately without knowing why they happen. Establishing deeper understanding of when the behaviors are more or less likely to occur is somewhat more difficult. Knowing why they occur is quite difficult. Different psychologists might observe the same behavior but develop very different explanations as to why the behavior takes place.

To have confidence in psychological research, investigators insist that the research be objective, that is, clearly defined and described. In addition, conclusions have to be data driven; that is, the results of the study rather than opinion should determine any conclusions drawn. It is also important that research be verifiable; that is, other psychologists should be given enough detail to repeat a study to see if the same results occur. Finally, the research needs to be made public so that it can undergo scrutiny by independent researchers. If all of these conditions are met, scientists will be more confident that the outcome of research is valid.

To get good answers to the research questions, psychologists use many different approaches to research. Some of those approaches involve observing what naturally occurs, whereas other approaches make use of manipulation of a situation to study the effect of manipulation. When the researcher actively changes the environment to see how behaviors change, it is possible to draw causal conclusions.

When psychological research involves humans, one complicating factor involves the cultural groups to which people belong. Culture can exert a significant effect on the outcome of research because culture has a notable impact not only on behavior and attitude but also on the way that people think. As a result, comparisons across cultures are often difficult to make because it might not be clear whether differences are due to treatments that psychologists implement or to culture.

Further Reading

Bensley, D. Alan. *Critical Thinking In Psychology: A Unified Skills Approach*. Belmont, CA US: Thomson Brooks/Cole Publishing Co, 1998.

Matsumoto, David. *Cultural Influences on Research Methods and Statistics*. Long Grove, IL US: Waveland Press.

Stanovich, Keith E. *How to Think Straight About Psychology* (7th ed.). Boston, MA US: Pearson.

CHAPTER 2

EXPERIMENTS IN PSYCHOLOGY

DETERMINING THE CAUSES OF BEHAVIOR

One of the goals of research is to find ways to control behavior, which may be the most difficult goal to achieve. Before you can exert control, you first need to be able to describe the behavior, predict when it will occur, and explain why it occurs when it does and why it is absent when it does not occur. Once you know this basic information, it is possible to create a situation in which the behavior is likely to happen.

Finding out what factors lead to a particular behavior is very difficult because any behavior can probably be caused by more than one factor. For example, people cry for very different reasons—because they are happy, because they are sad, because they are angry, because they are frustrated, and so forth. Thus, psychologists recognize that they may be able to identify the cause of a person's behavior in a particular situation, but they also know that in different circumstances, something else entirely might cause the same behavior.

Another aspect of trying to identify what causes a behavior is that two (or more) different forces acting at the same time may combine to cause a behavior that would not occur if only one of those forces were present. For instance, people are sometimes willing to work hard, but sometimes they are not. When people are working on a group project, it is pretty typical that all members of that group work less hard within the group than they would if each of them were working alone. This phenomenon is called social loafing.

Furthermore, it is more likely that people will engage in social loafing when they do not have a specific, meaningful task to perform. Thus, we can make a better prediction about how hard a person will work by knowing two things: (a) is the person working individually or in a group and (b) is the person's task meaningful?

Psychologists who are interested in knowing the cause of behavior prefer to conduct experiments involving systematic manipulation of situations in which such behavior tends to occur. With knowledge of the multiple factors that lead to a behavior, a researcher can control a situation to increase the chances that people will act in a desired way. But psychologists also recognize that people are complicated, so they cannot guarantee that their attempts at control of behavior will be successful all the time. Multiple factors affect behavior, and we cannot control all of them all the time.

REQUIREMENTS FOR DETERMINING CAUSES OF BEHAVIOR

It is sometimes tempting to conclude that when two events occur in close proximity, the first event caused the second. One of the most powerful examples of this line of reasoning involves the situation in which a person eats a particular food and then becomes sick shortly afterward. The person concludes that the food caused the illness (and the negative physiological response to that food in the future reinforces the person's belief). In reality, the person might have been coming down with something and would have become sick even if he or she had not eaten the food. Still, it feels real to this person that this particular food caused the sickness.

Along the same lines, consider someone working at a computer who installs a new piece of software. Shortly afterward, the computer crashes and will not function. The immediate response by the user is that he or she did something wrong by using the new software. That is, something about the new software must have caused the computer to crash. As is often the case, installation of the new software may be completely irrelevant. It is more than likely that the computer malfunctioned because of something internal to it, not because of what the user did.

These are good illustrations of what researchers mean when they say that "correlation does not imply causation." That is, just because two events occur close together in time, it does not necessarily mean that one caused the other. It may be the case that one did cause the other, but it is just as likely that one had nothing to do with the other. You simply cannot know for sure. It is this uncertainty about the causes of behavior that calls for experimental research that can resolve the ambiguity.

Scientists have identified three conditions that are required for gaining confidence in the conclusion that event A caused event B. If all three conditions are not met, we cannot be sure whether two events are causally related.

First, the two events have to occur together, which is called **covariance**. The causal event has to reliably predict the effect. But covariance is not enough to allow determination of cause and effect. For example, research has shown that depressed people experience fewer positive life experiences. It would be easy to conclude that the absence of positive events in a person's life leads to depression. If fact, maybe this is the case. On the other hand, it is also possible that when a person is depressed, he or she does not enter into situations that would lead to positive outcomes. So it is equally likely that the depression may be one cause of the small number of positive events.

What is true is that the two events covary. That is, they vary together reliably: Greater depression is accompanied by fewer positive events, and less depression is accompanied by more positive events. The pattern is predictable. But predictability is not sufficient for the conclusion that one causes the other.

A second requirement for determining cause and effect is **temporal precedence**. That is, the cause has to come first, and the effect has to follow it. It makes sense logically that there cannot be an effect without something to cause it first. So if we do not know which of two things occurred first, it is not possible to conclude that one of them is a causal agent.

The third requirement for a causal conclusion is **internal validity**. When internal validity exists, it means that you can identify one factor responsible for causing a behavior and can rule out all the others. If there are multiple forces that may be at work in causing behavior, it is impossible to identify which one or ones are important and which are irrelevant.

It is important to remember that in a given situation of causal ambiguity, event A may actually cause event B. So if a person eats the potato salad at a picnic and later gets sick, it may be the case that the potato salad really was to blame. The problem is that we do not know for sure. Although it is true that the two events covaried and also true that eating the food preceded the sickness, other possible causes cannot be ruled out, so the internal validity component has not been satisfied.

When psychologists conduct experimental research, they try to set up studies that ensure the three requirements for determining causation are met. Both the nature of experiments and the controlled testing involved must satisfy the three conditions needed to draw a conclusion of cause and effect.

THE DESIGN OF EXPERIMENTS

Even though some experiments become quite complicated, the logic of experimentation is quite simple. In the simplest version of an experiment, you have a group of participants or subjects that you separate into two groups on a random basis so that the two groups are pretty much comparable. Then you administer one treatment to the first group and a different treatment to the second group. If they behave differently after the treatments, the most likely explanation is that

Are Jokes Only as Funny as People Expect Them to Be?

Two researchers (Wimer & Beins, 2008) wanted to know if jokes have a constant level of funniness or if you can manipulate people so they rate the jokes either as more or less funny, depending on the experimental treatment. They took a group of people and randomly assigned them to one of two conditions that heard either that they should expect funny jokes or that they should expect jokes that were not very funny. The participants in the two groups rated the same jokes to see if expectations affected the ratings.

The results showed that the two messages indeed had different effects. The average ratings by the two groups differed. On a seven-point scale, people who expected funny jokes rated them half a point higher than people who expected jokes that were not very funny.

It appears that you can affect people's responses to humor by giving them a believable message. But a separate experiment revealed that people were not affected by an unrealistic message. When they heard that the jokes were supposedly hysterically funny or horribly unfunny (which they were not), the participants ignored the message entirely.

In this experiment, two comparable groups received different treatments. When they subsequently rated the jokes, the ratings moved in the direction of the expectations. Thus, the researchers were able to conclude that the different messages that the participants received caused a difference in the ratings.

Source: Wimer, David J., and Bernard C. Beins. 2008. Expectations and perceived humor. *Humor: International Journal of Humor Research* 21(3):347–363.

the treatments made a difference. That is, you can conclude that the treatments caused the differences in behavior.

Experimental Measurements

Psychologist E. L. Thorndike commented that "Anything that exists, exists in a certain quantity and can be measured." This is a fundamental tenet of science. If we cannot measure it, we cannot study it scientifically. One of the great challenges in psychology is that psychologists try to measure things that are hard to quantify. For example, how can we measure intelligence? We typically measure it through a standardized intelligence test like the Stanford-Binet. Unfortunately, such tests measure how much people have learned, not some underlying characteristic of the test takers.

Over the decades, psychologists have tried to measure intelligence in a variety of ways, including how quickly people respond to a stimulus, how big their heads (and, presumably, their brains) are, how quickly they can assemble puzzles, whether they know the definitions of words, and even how long they can stand on tiptoes. Some of these measuring factors turned out to be of no use, but some were quite useful in predicting behaviors.

As a rule, we are forced to measure intelligence indirectly because it is not a tangible thing. Psychologists refer to intelligence as a **hypothetical construct**, which is a concept that we cannot observe directly but that we believe is useful in helping us understand behavior. In the case of intelligence, it seems clear that more intelligent people can do more than less intelligent people. So intelligence might be a useful concept in explaining why one person learns more quickly than another person.

The question in dealing with hypothetical constructs is how to measure them, something that psychologists continually grapple with. For example, we measure depression by giving a test that asks about behaviors we associated with the concept of depression. For research purposes, psychologists might ask people to respond how accurately certain phrases describe them: "I have a low opinion of myself" (with which a depressed person would agree) or "I am very pleased with myself" (with which a depressed person would disagree). Such questions let psychologists know about the effects of depression, but the questions do not actually measure depression itself. And the measurements are only as good as the questions, so if researchers do not use the right questions, their assessments are not likely to be valid.

Because so many of the concepts that psychologists deal with are abstract and pertain to processes hidden in the brain, researchers must make use of indirect measurements that they hope will tap into those hidden processes. Fortunately, even though we do not know exactly what intelligence, depression, learning, motivation, and so forth really are, psychologists have developed useful and practical techniques to measure what we think they are. These measurements have led to some very interesting and very useful outcomes.

Experimental Variables

Like other scientists, psychologists measure the things that interest them. The psychological constructs that they measure are present in different degrees across a group of people. When a trait or condition can take on different values, it is referred to as a **variable**.

One highly studied personality variable is extraversion, the degree to which a person is outgoing with and around others. If researchers want to know what other characteristics are associated with the variable of extraversion, they will administer a personality inventory to a group of people and measure some other trait or behavior, then assess the degree to which these are related. The next sidebar illustrates how psychologists sometimes measure extraversion.

In one study, a group of researchers put participants either in a good mood or in a neutral mood to see if mood led to differences in creativity and learning ability. They also wanted to know whether extraverts differed from introverts. The results indicated that a good mood facilitated creativity in people with high, but not low, extraversion scores; the good mood hampered the ability to recall a set of words for everybody, regardless of their degree of extraversion.

When psychologists conduct an experiment, they manipulate a variable called the **independent variable**. In the example above, the independent variable was the mood (positive or neutral) that the researchers induced in the participants. They also grouped the participants into high extraversion and low extraversion groups based on their scores on a personality inventory to create a second independent variable.

Sometimes researchers cannot manipulate variables experimentally. They cannot, for example, make an extraverted person become introverted or vice versa. People come to studies the way they are, so researchers may simply create groups of people that share characteristics appropriate for those groups. As you

How Can You Measure the Personality Variable of Extraversion?

Some people are outgoing; others are shy. Researchers have found that extraversion is reliably associated with certain behaviors and characteristics. For example, extraverts show an increase in creativity when they are in a good mood compared to a neutral mood, they can be more effective salespeople than intraverts, and when they plan to engage in physical exercise, they tend to do so.

The question is how to measure the internal, psychological characteristic of extraversion. Table 2.1 contains ten items from an inventory that psychologists have used to measure the trait and how they come up with the measurement.

As you can see, some items are positively keyed, which means that a higher score on that item is associated with greater extraversion. Some items are negatively keyed, which means that higher scores are associated with less extraversion; for these items, psychologists use *reverse scoring* so that in getting the person's total score, higher numbers are always associated with greater extraversion. On this scale, the person responds with a number on a scale of 1 (*Does not describe me accurately*) to 5 (*Describes me accurately*). On a negatively keyed item, if a person responded with a 1, the score would be changed to a 5; a 2 would be changed to a 4, and so forth. In this example, the person's score on the extraversion variable would be a 42, which would reflect a fairly high level.

will see below, researchers can draw different types of conclusions depending on whether they randomly assign study participants to a group or whether they use a preexisting characteristic to decide how to group participants.

After creating the groups, the researchers measured the participants' creativity in problem solving and the number of words from a list of 15 that participants could remember after seeing them once. The goal was to determine if performance was affected by mood and by level of extraversion. These measurements of performance constitute the **dependent variable**, which is a measurement whose value may depend on the independent variable—i.e., does a person's level of creativity depend on the person's mood.

To measure creativity in this study, the researchers presented participants with three words, and the participants had to come up with a fourth word that related to the first three. For example, for *Falling-Actor-Dust*, a related word would be *Star*. Because creativity is an internal characteristic (like extraversion or depression), measurement must be indirect, specifically, by means of a behavioral task that is related to creative behavior. On the other hand, the

TABLE 2.1
Psychological Characteristics of Extraversion

Item	Keying	Example of a Person's Response	How the Item Would Be Scored
Am the life of the party	Positive	4	4
Feel comfortable around people	Positive	5	5
Start conversations	Positive	3	3
Talk to a lot of different people at parties	Positive	4	4
Don't mind being the center of attention	Positive	3	3
Don't talk a lot	Negative	2	4
Keep in the background	Negative	1	5
Have little to say	Negative	1	5
Don't like to draw attention to myself	Negative	2	4
Am quiet around strangers	Negative	1	5
Total Extraversion Score			**42**

variable of learning is directly measurable. The researchers simply counted the number of words that each person remembered.

POTENTIAL PROBLEMS IN RESEARCH
Extraneous Variables and Confounds

In an experiment, the researcher manipulates one or more variables to see how behavior changes. The hope is to be able to identify the reasons, or causes, for any differences in behavior across groups. Sometimes, however, there are factors at work that the experimenter does not know about but that affect behavior. These factors are known as **extraneous variables**.

For example, a group of researchers discovered that children who had night lights in their bedrooms when they were very young were more likely to become nearsighted than were children who did not have night lights. The researchers concluded that children needed periods of darkness for the development of normal vision and that night lights were problematic. The researchers believed that they had identified a possible cause for nearsightedness.

It was clearly the case that children who had had night lights tended to become nearsighted. These two features covaried, which is critical for determining causation. And the night lights preceded the nearsightedness, so the supposed cause preceded the effect.

A problem arose with the internal validity criterion, however. It turned out that the nearsighted children generally had nearsighted parents; this is not surprising because nearsightedness has a genetic component. It was likely that nearsighted parents needed the night lights to be able to see in the dark, but it was not the presence of night lights that led to nearsightedness. It was the genetic connection. Subsequent research that controlled for the extraneous variable of parental vision showed that night lights do not lead to nearsightedness.

A particular type of extraneous variable that systematically affects one group but does not affect the rest of the groups is called a **confound**. One example is illustrated by a study on fear of failure. Researchers showed female participants a picture of a woman studying and showed male participants a picture of a man studying. The woman was called Jane and the man John. The participants' task was to make up a story about the picture. Invariably, women told more negative stories, and men more positive stories. The researchers concluded that women showed a fear of failure that was reflected in their negative stories.

For decades researchers continued to conduct research like this, asking participants to describe female and male characters. In order to make the differences between the female and male condition as similar as possible, the investigators changed the names as little as possible, pairing Jane and John or using other names that varied little from one other. As it turns out, the female names tended to be perceived by female participants as old fashioned or associated with negative personality characteristics compared to the male names.

So participants seemed to be responding to the names of the characters more than to need for achievement or fear of failure. When researchers removed the confound and chose names comparable in desirability, women as a group no longer showed fear of failure. Recent research shows that attitudes predict fear of failure better than gender.

Participant and Experimenter Effects

Any time two or more people come together, it is a social situation. So although it might seem that laboratory experiments are not really social situations, they are. People pay attention to social cues and act accordingly. In connection with this, psychologists have found that a researcher's mood can affect the way participants respond during an experiment. Psychologists Robert Rosenthal and Ralph Rosnow have identified several effects that relate to the social nature of an experimental setting.

When people respond to the way an experimenter acts, they are showing **psychosocial effects**. For example, researchers who have a high need for social approval act differently toward participants than researchers whose need for social approval is low. They may smile more, or they may stand closer to a study participant. Such behaviors may influence the participant's responses during the study.

Sometimes participants are affected by an experimenter's physical characteristics, including age, sex, or race. In this situation, changes in behavior are the result of something psychologists call **biosocial effects**. It is important to remember that the effects are not caused by biology. The term *biosocial* in this

Psychological Misnomer

The Hawthorne effect is widely known and appears in many textbooks on psychology. Changes in behavior occur rather predictably when people know somebody is watching them. The name of this phenomenon, however, is a misnomer arising from a series of studies at a factory in Hawthorne, Illinois, in which people changed their behaviors in response to different conditions. Historians of psychology have shown that the behavior changes actually occurred for reasons very different from what we now know as the Hawthorne effect.

The real causes included the substitution of highly productive employees in the research as replacements for the people who were not very good workers. As a result, in some studies when productivity increased, it was because of personnel changes, not to an experimental manipulation or to the fact that the employees took pride in being part of a research project.

context refers to supposedly "natural" characteristics of the researcher rather than psychological characteristics.

It is also possible that participants' behavior can be affected by reasons having little to do with the researcher. A phenomenon associated with behavior changes in participants is the **Hawthorne effect**, the tendency for people to change their behaviors simply because they are being observed.

Another reason for behavior change related to factors that are not relevant to a given experiment is called evaluation apprehension, which is somewhat similar to the Hawthorne effect but is specifically characterized by the discomfort people feel when they think that somebody is observing them. Evaluation apprehension can have negative effects on behavior. One well-known phenomenon that illustrates this is stereotype threat. When women are in the presence of men, for example, they may perform less well on math problems than they would if there were no men present because of a widely believed cultural stereotype that men are better at math than women are. Likewise, men may do less well on math problems if they think they are being compared with people who are supposed to be more proficient in math, like Asians (men or women). It does not matter that the researcher or members of another group are not engaging in behavior or making comments that seem judgmental—what matters is what the participant believes and how that belief affects behavior.

Control of Potential Problems
Random Assignment
There are several aspects of control that are important in experiments that lead to valid conclusions about cause and effect. First, the researchers have to document that the experimental manipulation associated with creating different treatment groups reliably led to different outcomes; this is associated with the covariance requirement for establishing cause and effect. The researchers must also apply the treatments before measuring the outcome, which relates to the temporal precedence rule. What remains now is to satisfy the internal validity requirement. That is, the researchers have to demonstrate that their manipulation was the only likely cause of the differences in the behaviors of the people in the various treatment groups.

One of the first steps in establishing internal validity is by **random assignment** of participants to conditions. By randomly placing the participants in Group A or in Group B, the researchers are likely to have two groups that are not systematically different to begin with. That is, if the assignment to condition is random, it is unlikely that all of the smart people or all of the highly motivated people end up in the same group. So if the study involves learning, people who are likely to be motivated or unmotivated learners are distributed across both groups pretty evenly.

Suppose the researchers placed all the early arrivers in one group and the late arrivers in a different group in a learning experiment. It is very reasonable to believe that the highly motivated people arrived first, so if that group performed well on a learning task, it might be due to their motivation level rather than because of the experimental treatment.

Psychologists have asked whether depression affects a person's memory and have found that depressed people often show memory impairment. But that kind of research does not involve true experiments because the investigators cannot randomly assign people to a depressed condition or to a nondepressed condition. So any differences in memory between depressed and nondepressed people may be related to factors other than depression. In fact, if a person's memory is very deficient, that might itself be a contributing cause of depression. In addition, neurological damage to the brain could lead both to depression and to decreased memory. So this kind of study can show the pattern of depression as being associated with poorer memory functions but cannot establish that depression is the cause of memory deficits.

To deal with these problems, psychologists have developed ways of creating temporary states of depressed mood in people. One method is to ask people to remember depressing events in their lives; a second method involves having people look at negative photographs (e.g., starvation); a third approach is to have people repeat negative statements (e.g., I'm discouraged and unhappy about myself). All three of these techniques are useful in altering people's moods, putting them in a state resembling mild (and temporary) depression. For ethical reasons, it is important that the effects be short lived; researchers do not want people leaving their laboratories in a worse emotional state than the one in which they arrived. Fortunately, these techniques have predictable effects that do not last very long.

With these techniques, researchers can randomly assign people to each of the conditions associated with the independent variable: the depressed condition and the nondepressed condition. This assignment procedure gives researchers confidence that the two groups are more or less comparable at the start of the study. The question is whether they behave the same or differently after the experimental treatments. The sidebar on page 28 describes some memory research using a mild, induced state resembling depression.

Single- and Double-Blind Studies

Psychologists have discovered other potential problems that can occur in experiments. For example, when participants engage in a mood-altering task, they may pick up on cues about the purpose of the experiment and, trying to be "good" participants, they conform to what they think the researcher expects of them. So if they think that they should act as if they were in a negative mood state, they may do so even if they are feeling very positive at the time. In such instances, psychologists say that participants are responding to the **demand characteristics** of the study.

There are several possible solutions to this kind of problem. For an example related to the mood induction study, one solution is to see if the manipulation is working by recording behaviors that would be associated with a particular mood but that participants would not know about. If those behaviors appear, the investigator can assume that a person is actually in the desired mood state. For instance, researchers have found that naturally depressed people have lower pain tolerance than nondepressed people; people with a laboratory-induced version of mild depression show the same pattern that naturally depressed

Does Mood Affect Memory?

Several research projects have shown that people with depression sometimes show poorer memory than those without depression. In addition, research has revealed that mood can affect what a person remembers. Two researchers randomly assigned participants to either the negative mood group or the positive mood group, then used an experimental manipulation to induce the mood. Participants read such statements as *I'm so hopeless that I will never be a success* to prime them for the negative condition and *My future looks bright and promising* to prime them for the positive condition. In this study, the independent variable was the participant's mood state.

After the participants were in the appropriate mood state, they responded to questions like *Press the button when you can recall a specific time you experienced. . .* followed by a negative experience (like *a broken promise*) or a positive experience (like *an unexpected gift*). The researchers measured how long it took participants to respond. The dependent variable was the participant's response time.

The results showed that people in the negative state were quicker to respond to the negative event (e.g., the broken promise) than to the positive event, whereas those in the positive state were quicker to respond to the positive event than to the negative event. Figure 2.1 shows the pattern.

It is pretty obvious that mood did affect the participants' memories. In this experiment, participants were quick to retrieve memories that matched their current mood state. Numerous other studies have generated similar findings about enhanced recall of information that matches a person's emotional state. One potential implication is that people who are depressed may be prone to remembering negative events in their lives, which may in turn lead to a continued negative emotional state.

people do. In addition, people with natural and laboratory-induced depression show similarities in the way they walk, which differs from the way nondepressed people walk. Gauging by these and similarly observable phenomena, there is reason to believe that the mood-induction techniques are doing what researchers hope.

There are various other ways that researchers try to avoid demand characteristics in general. One way involves keeping participants ignorant of the condition they are in. Such a research design is known as a **single-blind study**. Of course, if the experimenter knows what condition the participant is in, the researcher might inadvertently convey cues about behavior to the participant. One way to preclude this is for researchers to create a **double-blind study** in

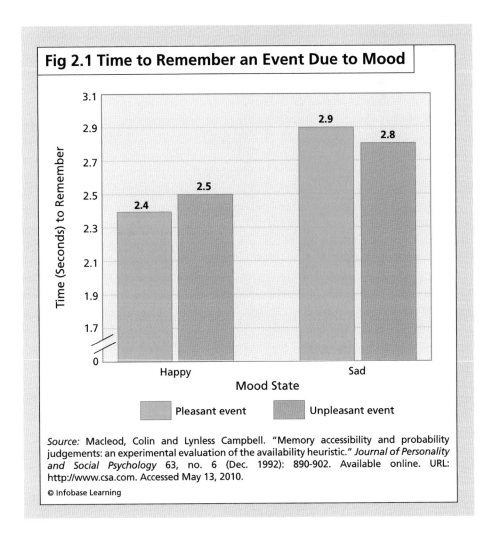

Fig 2.1 Time to Remember an Event Due to Mood

Source: Macleod, Colin and Lynless Campbell. "Memory accessibility and probability judgements: an experimental evaluation of the availability heuristic." *Journal of Personality and Social Psychology* 63, no. 6 (Dec. 1992): 890-902. Available online. URL: http://www.csa.com. Accessed May 13, 2010.

© Infobase Learning

which neither the participant nor the researcher knows the condition for a given participant. This strategy keeps the participant from figuring out the purpose of the study and the researcher from communicating important clues about expected behavior.

Another approach is to generate a **cover story** that will deflect the participant's attention away from the purpose of the research. In recent years, another solution has been to automate the research procedures. Historically, the experimenter almost always had to be physically present to administer the research protocol. But with the advent of computers, it is now easier to set up the procedure so that there is minimal chance that the participant and experimenter communicate information that would jeopardize the validity of the results.

Placebo and Control Groups

Sometimes an experimenter creates a group that believes it is getting a treatment but is not. This is called a **placebo group**. In studies of treatments for clinical depression, for example, participants who receive medication know they are taking something designed help them relieve their depression. Knowing they are being treated with medication, they may improve simply because they believe they should. So researchers may administer an inactive pill to make some participants think they are getting the medication. If there are placebo effects, both groups should improve. Investigations have shown that much of the benefit that patients show from medication for depression is actually a placebo effect.

In psychiatric research regarding medications, placebos may be viable. But in some psychological research, it is not feasible to administer something that looks like a treatment but is not. So researchers may use a **control group** instead—a group that receives no treatment and is simply measured with respect to the dependent variable. A control group may involve a manipulation that has a known effect so that the researcher can assess the effects of a new manipulation by comparing it to the old.

CONCLUSION

Experimental designs are useful for identifying the causes of a behavior. Researchers systematically manipulate an independent variable to see how changes in that variable affect a behavior, which is called the dependent variable. With appropriate controls, a psychologist can identify cause-and-effect relations between variables.

The three conditions that must be met in order for a researcher to conclude that there is a causal relation between variables are that the supposed cause has to vary predictably with the supposed effect, the cause must come before the effect, and other possible causes have to be ruled out. Unless these three conditions are satisfied, there is causal ambiguity.

Sometimes a researcher's physical or psychological characteristics can affect a respondent's behavior. This is an undesirable effect because the experimenter might not know about the participant's reactions, assuming that a participant's behavior is the result of the independent variable. In other cases, there may be design flaws in a study that can alter the results. Psychologists work diligently to try and eliminate such unwanted effects.

Further Reading

MacLeod, Colin, and Lynlee Campbell. 1992. Memory accessibility and probability judgments: An experimental evaluation of the availability heuristic. *Journal of Personality and Social Psychology* 63, (6) (Dec):890–902.

Wimer, David J., and Bernard C. Beins. 2008. Expectations and perceived humor. *Humor: International Journal of Humor Research* 21, (3):347–363.

CHAPTER 3

CORRELATIONS: SEARCHING FOR RELATIONSHIPS IN RESEARCH

Psychological research involves a wide variety of approaches. One common approach in studying complex relationships among different variables is the correlational research design. In such research, psychologists do not manipulate variables to see their effect on behavior. Rather, researchers measure behaviors of interest as they naturally occur.

This approach lets investigators study complex patterns of behavior. The advantage is that the research involves the behavior or mental processes of people doing what they normally do or think rather than seeing what happens in an artificially manipulated environment. One disadvantage is that the actual causes of behavior remain hidden. Psychologists who study complex social issues or who investigate complicated issues of personality are likely to use correlational designs because such designs can reveal the interplay of the many factors that affect people.

CORRELATIONAL RESEARCH

Psychologists recognize that certain traits and characteristics often go together. For example, people experiencing depression can also be prone to addictive behaviors. When researchers face issues as complex as these, it is very difficult to come up with explanations as to whether one causes the other. For ethical and other practical reasons, researchers cannot conduct experiments in which they induce clinical depression in people to see if depression is a causal factor for addictive behavior. In addition, it is likely that there is more than one contributing factor for each of these conditions. So the researchers rely on a **corre-lational design**, a strategy that differs from the experimental approach in which a small number of variables are controlled and manipulated so the psychologist can identify a cause. Rather, correlational designs show patterns or relationships among different variables. Sometimes correlational studies permit researchers to make useful predictions even if they do not know the actual causes of the behaviors that they predict.

In some correlational research, the investigators collect data themselves. They recruit participants and measure variables of interest. One group of researchers led by K.V. Petrides administered personality inventories and a test of emotional intelligence to participants. They found that emotional intelligence was positively correlated with levels of extraversion, conscientiousness, agree-ableness, and openness, and negatively correlated to neuroticism. People high on the first four traits showed more emotional intelligence than people low on these traits, with the pattern being reversed for the trait of neuroticism. The advantage of collecting your own data is that you can tailor your methodology so it answers the exact question you want to ask.

In contrast, you might use somebody else's data set that could have a larger and more diverse sample than you could reasonably obtain on your own. In other correlational research, investigators make use of existing data. Research-ers in the United States and in Canada, for example, have access to data from a regularly conducted, randomized survey of the populations of those coun-tries. This General Social Survey (GSS) contains questions about a wide range of social issues. A group of psychologists was interested in the factors that pre-dicted physical violence in intimate relationships. They used responses from a previously administered survey and found that childhood sexual abuse and either physical or mental disability predicted victimization in such relation-ships. One advantage of using existing data is ease of obtaining large amounts of data. A disadvantage is that a researcher using such data must rely on some-body else's questions, which may not focus on the researcher's specific interests.

RESEARCHING COMPLEX SOCIAL ISSUES

Research on complex social issues generally involves correlational designs because it is impractical or maybe even impossible to conduct a true experi-ment. A good example involves the issues addressed by the above-mentioned GSS. Researchers created the GSS in 1972 and have administered it periodically ever since. So there is a large collection of data from random samples of the population of the United States and a different set of samples for Canada.

Questions on the U.S. version of the GSS cover a wide range of topics, some dealing with very important social issues and some with relatively minor issues. Questions on important social issues might ask whether an employer offers heath insurance to the person completing the survey, whether the person believes that abortion is wrong, or whether the person would vote for a woman for president. Other, less weighty questions might ask whether the respondent believes that astrology is a real science or whether life is exciting or dull.

The issues addressed in the GSS are complex and often do not lend themselves to experimental analysis. Instead, researchers examine the responses to determine whether variables are related. So, for example, an investigator might be interested in learning whether there is an association between the frequency with which people attend religious services and opinions (pro or con) about whether scientists should be allowed to conduct research that causes pain in animals. According to the 2008 GSS data set, correlational analysis reveals that there is a very weak relation between attending religious services and attitudes about research causing pain in animals. Thus, only a general conclusion might be drawn from the data: The more often a person attends religious services, the less likely he or she believes that such research is acceptable But because the relationship between the two issues is so weak, it would be impossible to make a very good prediction about how any single person feels about the issue of animal research based solely on that person's religious behavior.

CORRELATION VERSUS CAUSATION

One of the strengths of correlational research is that it lets psychologists investigate complex patterns of thought and behavior. It would be hard to conceive of an experimental manipulation that would let a researcher determine if religious beliefs are a causal factor in a person's attitude toward research. But it is possible to spot the relationship even without knowing why a person holds a particular belief. Knowing how different variables relate to one another can lead to useful predictions. Researchers, for example, have studied variables related to the likelihood that a criminal will commit another crime in the future; the results from such studies can have significant practical value.

As noted above, one important limitation of correlational research is that it does not lend itself to causal conclusions. This restriction relates to the three criteria associated with determining causation. The factors must covary, the cause must precede the effect, and the researcher needs to be able to rule out factors other than the ones of interest. Depending on the particular variables, any of these three criteria could be the limiting factor that impedes (or precludes) a researcher's efforts to draw a causal conclusion.

For example, researchers have shown that robbery victims, who are often highly aroused emotionally by the crime, can recall the event in greater detail than can victims of fraud, which leads to less emotional arousal. These data could make it easy to assume that the heightened emotional response led to better memory for details about a robbery. In this example, the supposed cause (emotional arousal) occurs before the effect (the recall); in addition, the two factors (emotional response and memory) covary in the sense that the people in the aroused state remember more and those not so aroused remember less. The problem here is with internal validity because the presence of other factors that might lead to better or worse memory has not been determined.

One reason for the better memory about robbery may be that victims of robbery are generally interviewed soon after the crime and fraud victims are not. So it could very well be that the passage of time interferes with the memories of victims of fraud. Emotional arousal may have nothing to do with it.

There are, indeed, numerous complexities associated with determining causation. As the example about robbery and fraud indicates, a correlational pattern might reflect underlying causation, but all too often there isn't enough information to confirm that determination. One way that researchers approach

What Is the Correlation Between Media Violence and Aggression?

The correlation between exposure to violence in the media is well established. Numerous studies have shown that people who view violence on television and in the movies are more likely to be violent than people who are not exposed to media violence. As Figure 3.1 shows, the correlation between media violence and aggression is greater than many well-known relationships between variables and not much smaller than that between smoking and lung cancer. But these data do not make it clear that causation is involved. It might be that watching violent movies leads to the violent behavior, but it might be equally true that the attitude of people who are prone to violence leads them to watch such movies. Or it might be that there is some third variable that we do not know about that affects the causal connection between media violence and violent behavior. To get a clearer picture of cause and effect between these factors, investigators have conducted laboratory experiments under controlled conditions.

As it turns out, the correlational studies outside the laboratory and the experimental studies in the laboratory led to the same conclusion. So in spite of the respective limitations of laboratory experiments (i.e., they involve artificial situations) and of correlational studies (i.e., you cannot draw causal conclusions) by themselves, psychologists were able to reach some rather definitive conclusions by using both types of research, thus overcoming the limitations of each individual approach. The association between exposure to violence and aggressiveness is in fact so reliable that six major organizations that deal with physical and psychological health issues have issued a statement that exposure to violence in the media is the cause of actual violence.

this problem is to combine correlation findings with experimental findings. The illustration of the correlation between exposure to violence in the media and violent behavior in the sidebar presented below shows how psychologists combined correlational and experimental findings to help draw a conclusion about cause and effect.

Two specific problems that prevent researchers from determining causation are directionality and the presence of a third variable. **Directionality** is a problem that surfaces when there are two variables in a correlational study and it is not clear which of these is the cause and which is the effect. As explained in the discussion on violence and exposure to media violence, either one could, in theory, cause the other. Violent people might choose violent movies, or violent

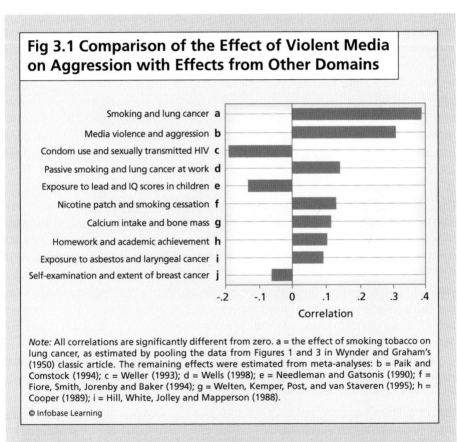

Fig 3.1 Comparison of the Effect of Violent Media on Aggression with Effects from Other Domains

Smoking and lung cancer **a**
Media violence and aggression **b**
Condom use and sexually transmitted HIV **c**
Passive smoking and lung cancer at work **d**
Exposure to lead and IQ scores in children **e**
Nicotine patch and smoking cessation **f**
Calcium intake and bone mass **g**
Homework and academic achievement **h**
Exposure to asbestos and laryngeal cancer **i**
Self-examination and extent of breast cancer **j**

-.2   -.1   0   .1   .2   .3   .4
Correlation

Note: All correlations are significantly different from zero. a = the effect of smoking tobacco on lung cancer, as estimated by pooling the data from Figures 1 and 3 in Wynder and Graham's (1950) classic article. The remaining effects were estimated from meta-analyses: b = Paik and Comstock (1994); c = Weller (1993); d = Wells (1998); e = Needleman and Gatsonis (1990); f = Fiore, Smith, Jorenby and Baker (1994); g = Welten, Kemper, Post, and van Staveren (1995); h = Cooper (1989); i = Hill, White, Jolley and Mapperson (1988).

© Infobase Learning

Source: Adapted from Bushman, Brad J., and Craig A. Anderson. 2001. Media violence and the American public: Scientific facts versus media misinformation. *American Psychologist* 56, (6-7) (Jun-Jul):477–489. Copyright 2001 American Psychological Association. Reprinted with permission.

movies may make a person prone to violence. If there is causation, the direction of causation is not clear.

The second problem is the **third-variable problem.** It might be the case that an unknown third variable is the cause and both other variables are effects. Sometimes researchers try to account for potential third variables, but it is always possible to miss the actual causal variable.

An example illustrating the directionality and third-variable problem concerns a group of researchers led by Katherine Presnell who addressed the relation between depression and bulimia, a disorder marked by excessive eating followed by some behavior (e.g., vomiting) designed to counteract the eating. They (and other psychologists) found that depression may lead to bulimia or that bulimia may lead to depression but that the relationships between these two factors (in either direction) were weak. Although each factor apparently affected the other, the impact of one on the other was slight. Moreover, the directionality problem may be at work here because bulimia and depression may have a causal relation but it is virtually impossible to determine which (if either) is the cause and which (if either) is the effect. In addition, there are numerous variables that are potential candidates for causing both disorders. The researchers speculated on some likely third variables, such as body dissatisfaction, low tolerance for distress, and a lack of social support. These factors, in fact, have been implicated in both disorders. To complicate matters even further, research is likely to show that both disorders have multiple causes that interact with one another.

PATTERNS OF CORRELATIONS

The relation between two variables is measured with a statistic called a **correlation coefficient**, often referred to simply as a correlation. The details can get complicated but, essentially, a strong relation between variables means that if you know the value of one variable, you have a sense of the value of the other variable. On the other hand, if there is a weak correlation between variables, the value of one is a less reliable predictor of the other. If there is no relation between two variables, one of them is not systematically predictable from the other.

When researchers compute correlation coefficients, the resulting values range from a maximum of +1.0 to a minimum of -1.0. In assessing the strength of a relationship between two variables, researchers use the absolute value of the correlation. So correlations of +.6 and -.6, for example, reflect equally strong associations between variables.

In a general sense, researchers identify correlations coefficients as being positive, negative, or zero. In a positive correlation between pairs of scores, if the score on variable 1 is low, the score on variable 2 will also be low. Similarly, if the score on variable 1 is high, the score on variable 2 will also be high. With a negative correlation, the pattern of paired scores is oppositional, meaning that if the score on one variable is low, the score on the other variable is high and vice versa.

As an example, consider the case of people who are trying to quit smoking. The success rate for smokers who want to stop is generally quite low, under 10 percent, so researchers search for factors that are related to a positive outcome. One group of psychologists led by Xiaomeng Xu conducted a study in which participants kept a record of so-called self-expanding events, such as an outstanding personal achievement or falling in love with someone. Participants were also asked to record the length of time they were able to abstain from smoking.

The research revealed a positive correlation between the number of self-expanding events that could lead to personal growth and the number of days

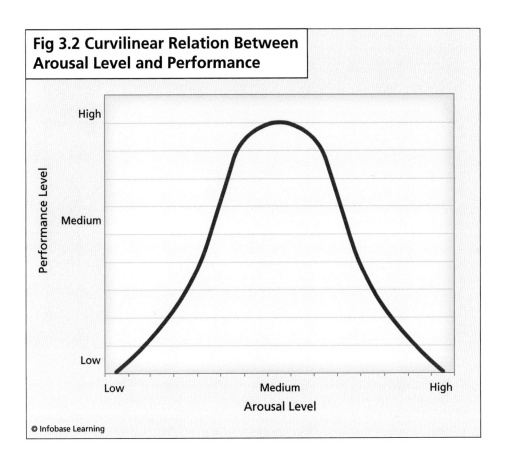

Fig 3.2 Curvilinear Relation Between Arousal Level and Performance

© Infobase Learning

The Connection Between Alcohol Consumption and Subsequent Problems

Most people are aware that it is a bad idea to drive a car after consuming alcohol because of the danger of accidents that may lead to injury or death. States have laws defining the maximum blood alcohol level permitted for legal driving; if a person's blood alcohol level exceeds a certain value, that person is deemed to be impaired or intoxicated. But even lower blood alcohol levels can lead to various problems.

A group of psychologists analyzed survey data from 8,698 college students about the amount of alcohol the students had consumed in the past four weeks and how many problems had resulted from the drinking. Problems ranged from fairly minor, like experiencing a hangover, to more serious, like trouble with the police. The researchers reported the number of problems as a function of how many drinks the student had consumed.

Damaged vehicle with anti-drinking and driving message. *(Wikipedia)*

of abstention from smoking. More personal growth was associated with greater abstinence; people who experienced fewer self-expanding events were less successful at quitting. The study was correlational, so it is not possible to determine that the presence of self-expanding events itself led to less smoking. Only an

There was a curvilinear relation between number of drinks and number of problems. Even after only one or two drinks, students said they had experienced problems. That is, even light drinking was associated with problems. But with three drinks, the number of problems rose very quickly and then kept going up, but at a slower rate.

The researchers pointed out that the relation between problems and number of drinks was complicated by whether the person was a light, moderate, or heavy drinker and whether the person was female or male. But the correlational analysis revealed a curvilinear pattern that held up across a wide variety of drinkers.

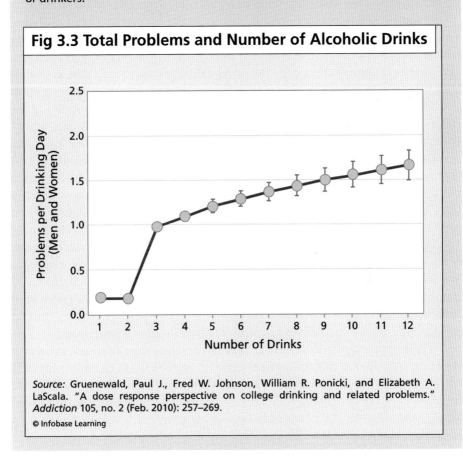

Fig 3.3 Total Problems and Number of Alcoholic Drinks

Source: Gruenewald, Paul J., Fred W. Johnson, William R. Ponicki, and Elizabeth A. LaScala. "A dose response perspective on college drinking and related problems." *Addiction* 105, no. 2 (Feb. 2010): 257–269.

© Infobase Learning

experimental design could do that. Nonetheless, as the researchers noted, the same reward centers of the brain are associated with self-expanding events and with the use of addictive substances like nicotine. So self-expanding events may substitute (to some degree) for some addictive drugs.

An example of research resulting in a negative correlation involved the degree to which young adolescents are victimized or bullied and their level of attachment with their parents. Psychologists Rachel Earl and Nicholas Burns discovered that children with greater attachment to their parents were less likely to be victimized whereas children who showed less attachment to their parents were more likely to be victims of bullying.

Many correlations that psychologists investigate are **linear correlations** in which a given increase in the score of one factor is associated with a constant level of change in the score of the other factor. So if the score on the first factor (whether high or low) is increased by amount X, the increase on the second factor (whether high or low) is by amount Y.

In some cases, a fixed amount of change on the first factor does not lead to a stable change on the second factor; the result is a **curvilinear** or **nonlinear relation**. One of the most well-known phenomena in psychology, the Yerkes-Dodson law, demonstrates a curvilinear relation. This law reveals that as arousal level increases, a person's performance on a task will improve up to a point at which further arousal leads worse performance. Psychologists studying the effect of alcohol consumption on problems encountered by college students have found a nonlinear pattern. Figure 3.2 on page 39 illustrates their research.

Researchers sometimes present correlational data using **scatter diagrams** that show the pattern of all the data points. If the correlation coefficient is positive, the trend is for scores on both variables to increase from low scores to high. A high, positive correlation with a value of +.75 appears in Figure 3.4 on page 43. A smaller, negative correlation of -.35 is depicted in Figure 3.5 on page 44. As you can see, the positive correlation shows a clear increase as the value of both variables increases. The pattern is reversed in the negative correlation. The line in each graph indicates the trend. For the positive correlation, the trend is upward from left to right; for the negative correlation, the trend is downward from left to right. The scatter diagram in Figure 3.6 on page 45 shows a data set in which the scores on variable 1 bear no relation to those on variable 2.

When correlation coefficients are relatively large, the scores on variable 2 tend not to be spread out for a given value of variable 1; on the other hand, if correlations are medium sized, you can see a trend (in Figure 3.5 it is a decrease from left to right), but the scores on the vertical axis tend to be more spread out for a given value on the horizontal axis. These graphs tell you that making a prediction about the score on variable Y is going to be more accurate for large correlations than for small.

Figure 3.6 shows a scatter diagram for a near-zero correlation. It is pretty obvious that if you select any point on the horizontal axis, the scores on the vertical axis are very different. The small correlation implies that it is difficult to make an accurate prediction of the score on variable 2 if you are given a score on variable 1.

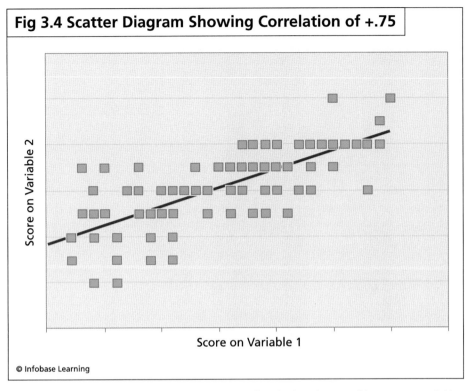

Fig 3.4 Scatter Diagram Showing Correlation of +.75

Score on Variable 2

Score on Variable 1

© Infobase Learning

Scatter diagram showing a correlation of +.75. The line depicts the rate of increase on variable 2 as the value of variable 1 increases.

Scatter diagrams will be look very different as the correlation grows or shrinks. With the maximum correlation of 1.0, for any single score on variable 1, scores on variable 2 will always be equal, and there will be regular and predictable changes as scores on variable 1 changes. The same predictability would exist for the smallest correlation coefficient possible, -1.0. As the strength of the correlation (i.e., its absolute value) diminishes in size, the spread of scores on variable 2 will increase for a single value on variable 2, meaning less predictability in the scores. As the correlation approaches zero, predicting the score on variable 2 when given a score on variable 1 becomes quite inaccurate.

FACTORS AFFECTING THE SIZE OF A CORRELATION

The most common correlation coefficient is called the Pearson correlation. It is useful in a wide range of research projects, but it does have some limitations. That is, there are situations that can arise in which there are predictable associations between variables that the Pearson correlation will not detect.

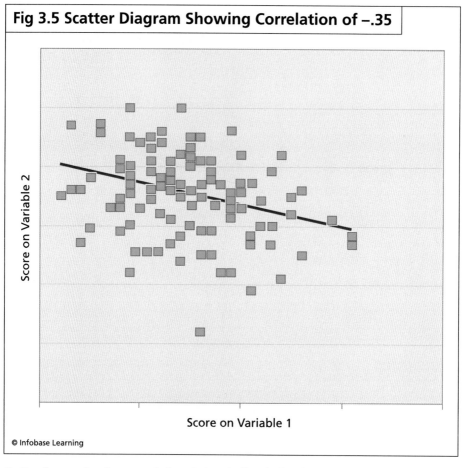

Fig 3.5 Scatter Diagram Showing Correlation of −.35

Score on Variable 2

Score on Variable 1

© Infobase Learning

Scatter diagram showing a correlation of -.35. The line depicts the rate of decrease for this negative correlation on variable 2 as the value of variable 1 increases.

For example, if two variables are not related in a linear fashion, the correlation coefficient will underestimate the degree to which two variables are associated. Figure 3.2, which shows a very predictable pattern, shows a connection between two variables that is curvilinear. The Pearson correlation would not be useful in this situation. The more a trend deviates from a straight line, the less valid the Pearson correlation.

A second situation in which the correlation coefficient gives less useful results involves data that show a small range of scores on at least one of the variables. Suppose the highest 50 percent of scores in Figure 3.4 were missing. The resulting scatter diagram would look like the one in Figure 3.6. The scatter of data points would become more circular, and data in a circular pattern reflect a low correlation. So there might be a real association between two variables,

Fig 3.6 Scatter Diagram Showing Correlation Near Zero

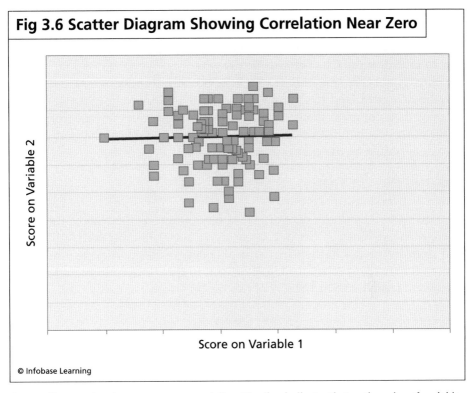

© Infobase Learning

Scatter diagram showing a near-zero correlation. The line indicates that as the value of variable 1 changes, there is no predictable change in the value of variable 2.

but if there is a restricted range of scores on a variable, the Pearson correlation would indicate a weak connection.

It is also possible that you might miss an association between variables if your data come from two groups that behave differently. For example, a group of investigators led by Manolis Markianos determined the cholesterol levels and the level of the neurotransmitter serotonin in a group of research participants because the combination of low cholesterol and low serotonin activity in the brain is associated with aggressiveness, violence, and suicidal behavior. The investigators were interested in seeing if there was a correlation between the levels of the two substances in their participants.

There was no correlation between the two variables. A low level of cholesterol, for instance, did not predict anything about serotonin activity. However, when the researchers separated their sample into males and females and computed separate correlation coefficients for the two groups, they found that there was a positive correlation between cholesterol and serotonin levels in men, but there was no correlation between the two for women. In this study, the two sexes showed different patterns; when the researchers mixed all of the participants into one large group for data analysis, the relation between cholesterol and serotonin was not apparent. This kind of result illustrates why it is important to investigate all data patterns very closely.

Finally, another situation in which supposedly accurate research findings may be deceptive (and inaccurate) relates to the presence of outliers, that is, extreme data points. If there are data points that are very deviant from most of the other data points, the correlation coefficient might be inflated or diminished, depending on the circumstances.

MAKING PREDICTIONS

When two variables are correlated, it is possible for psychologists to make predictions about the value of one variable if they know something about the other. There is, as explained earlier in this chapter, a correlation between SAT scores and students' grades in their first year of college. Colleges want to admit students who are likely to succeed, so they reason that if SAT scores and college grades are related, maybe the school can use SAT scores to predict college success. The statistics are complicated, but the correlation between SAT scores and first-year grade-point average (GPA) is between .5 and .6.

In order to enhance predictive success, colleges also factor in high school grade point average (HSGPA). Alone, HSGPA predicts college grades about as well as the SAT does. But if these two scores are combined, predictions become better. The correlation based on both SAT and HSGPA with college GPA is greater than .6.

Correlations like these are far from perfect, but they allow colleges to make reasonable predictions. As with any complex prediction, however, schools will make mistakes in admitting students who will not succeed and in not admitting students who would succeed. But this approach is much better than simply admitting students on a random basis.

It is pretty clear that there are many forces that can affect a student's performance in college classes: the difficulty of the classes, how much time the student spends preparing for classes and tests, the degree of social pressure that the student's friends exert, and so on. So it is no surprise that predictions about how well students will perform in school are imperfect. The college will make errors in selecting the students it accepts: It will admit students who appear capable of succeeding but do not or reject applicants who would have succeeded. Nonetheless, simple variables like high school grades and SAT scores are fairly accurate criteria; if those two scores are paired, the prediction gets better. In the end, the predictions that a college makes are better than a random admission policy. It is important to note that colleges recognize the limitations of using only these two predictors, so they also base part of their decisions on other factors, such as skills that the students have demonstrated or experiences that show initiative and determination.

When researchers use one variable to predict another, it is called **regression analysis**. If researchers use multiple variables, as colleges do in deciding whom to admit, the approach is called **multiple regression**.

One important factor to consider in making predictions involves trying to estimate a score for an individual person when numbers are based only on grouped data rather than on data at the individual level. For instance, studies of suicide across different nations tend to use data that reflect an entire country. When researchers have such grouped data, predictions about the likelihood that a single individual will commit suicide are not likely to be valid.

This type of problem involves what is known as the **ecological fallacy**, the use of predictions about an individual from a data set that does not use individualized data. People who fall victim to the ecological fallacy are assuming that every person in a group is at the average regarding the data. Naturally, people show a lot of variability, so assuming that any individual is average does not recognize such variability.

CONCLUSION

Correlational research is very useful for finding relationships among variables in complex situations. Researchers use correlational designs when they cannot manipulate an environment directly to assess cause and effect. As a result, the relationships among variables can be important and useful, but it is not possible to determine causal relationships with this kind of design.

Sometimes correlational patterns are positive such that when a score on one variable increases, so does the score on the other. Sometimes correlations are negative, in which case a score on one variable increases while the other decreases. When researchers discover reliable correlations, they can use them to make predictions about future behavior. In dealing with complex behaviors, psychologists recognize that their predictions will not be perfect. But the information they gain from correlational studies can be informative and useful.

Further Reading

Jones, Stephen. *Statistics in Psychology: Explanations Without Equations.* London, UK: Palgrave Macmillan, 2010.

CHAPTER 4

SURVEY RESEARCH

Surveys are a part of everyday life, involving topics as diverse as attitudes and opinions about life style choices, political preferences, and buying habits. Although people tend to take scientific surveys for granted, they are actually a fairly recent instrument for data gathering. Initial attempts to survey the U.S. populace began in earnest in the 1930s, but such surveys would not become scientifically valid until a couple decades later.

Historically, governments have collected data about the people they governed on a regular basis. This has been accomplished through a **census** that identified every person or household within the population. Naturally, this process was complex because a census taker would have to visit every household to see how many people lived there and what resources they possessed. (The censuses was often done so that rulers could determine how much they should tax each individual.)

The first census appears to have taken place in ancient Egypt about 5,000 years ago. Data from an ancient Chinese census of about 4,000 years ago still exists. Currently, many countries have a periodic census, although in poorer regions of the globe, the census may be intermittent at best. In the United States, the census is decennial (occurring every ten years), and every household is legally required to participate.

Beginning with the first U.S. census, there have been errors in the data, partly because finding every person in the country was simply not feasible. In the early years of the country, many people lived in remote and inaccessible areas, and some people simply did not want to be found. Today there are few inaccessible areas in the United States, but there are still people who do not want to be found. This includes (but is not limited to) people residing in the country without legal documentation and people who suspect that the government will use the census data against them.

Using assorted statistical techniques, researchers can do a more effective job of anticipating the movement of people in the country, identifying locations that will need more services (like hospitals or roads), and so forth. Statisticians have also developed ways to use statistical sampling to generate better estimates of the size of the population by supplementing actual counts. But although statistical sampling is an effective way to "find" people missed by the census, it is politically controversial because it does not actually involve counting every person, which is what the constitution specifies.

It is important to note that a census is only one example of data gathering by surveying. The biggest difference between a census and other surveys is that a census involves an entire population whereas most other surveys research only certain segments of a population As previously noted, there can be errors in census data; the same is true of all surveys. In conducting surveys, researchers hope to attain a sample that is representative of the broader population so that what they know about the sample is also true of that broader population. The investigators know, however, that they are working with estimates rather than quantifiable facts and figures; they also know that any time there are estimates, there is the possibility of error in their conclusions.

CONSIDERATIONS FOR CREATING VALID SCIENTIFIC SURVEYS

Some questionnaires are designed for scientific research, some for entertainment, and some to hide the fact that somebody is trying to sell something. In general, when social researchers or legitimate political pollsters conduct surveys, they let the respondent know who they are and the purpose of the research. In fact, the Council for Marketing and Opinion Research has developed an ethics code that specifies that all responses will remain anonymous and confidential. The ethics codes states that respondents are not to be sold anything or asked for money under the pretext of research.

In contrast, there are numerous nonscientific surveys, like those conducted by major political organizations or supermarkets (among others). The responses of people completing these surveys do not say anything useful about the attitudes or opinions of people in general. Many such surveys end with a request for a donation; others might push products they want consumers to buy. It is quite difficult to conduct scientific survey research well. Perhaps the most difficult aspect of creating a survey is constructing a questionnaire and specifically individual questions on that questionnaire. For many questionnaires (both scientific or not so scientific), wording has become relatively standard. For example, various surveys about political preferences might ask, "If the election were held today, would you vote for X or would you vote for Y?" But for survey research involving new topics, investigators must create questions, test them on a sample, and then revise them as needed. Small differences in wording can lead to significant differences in the way people respond. The way questions are sequenced can also affect the way people answer.

If the investigators want to know what people think about some topic, they need to deliver their questions to a sample of people who are representative of the population. So another issue researchers face is finding a sample that fits that description. After the researchers determine the format of the questions and the nature of the sample of respondents they plan to query, they must also decide on the means they will use to administer their survey. Current approaches to conducting survey research include contact by phone or by mail, face-to-face interviews, and the Internet.

THE ORIGINS OF QUESTIONNAIRES AND SURVEY RESEARCH

The use of questionnaires in psychological research preceded the modern theory and application of surveying techniques by several decades. Noted psychologist G. Stanley Hall and psychologists in his laboratory were among the first to make extensive use of questionnaires before the turn of the 20th century. Prior to Hall, investigators observed behaviors and recorded verbal reports of research participants. Hall changed that by creating questionnaires that he and his students used to study children's and students' thought processes. However, the way that these researchers used their questionnaires was quite unlike today's survey research. Hall used questionnaires in laboratory research with small convenience samples (using available, and therefore convenient, individuals or groups) rather than large-scale survey research of the type that exists today.

The first two listings of attitude research in the PsycINFO database focused on the belief in life after death. They appeared in the *Proceedings of the Society for Psychical Research*, which studied paranormal phenomena (and is now considered nonscientific), and in the *American Journal of Psychology*.

It is rather obvious that in the early decades of the 20th century, researchers were quite limited in the ways they could contact people. Most people did not have a telephone, and there was no Internet. So the only options were mail or in person. But administering surveys in person involved a lot of time and expense if the research was planning to involve a sample of respondents from a large or a geographically diverse population.

As a result, the most feasible approach to a national survey in the early years would have been by mail. But there were problems with this approach, too. The rate of illiteracy in rural areas was relatively high, so people in such areas would be missing from the sample. And there was another critical question. How would the researchers get the names and addresses of the people they were going to contact? Today there are companies who can provide mailing lists, but such companies did not exist back then. So the early researchers had to make the best judgments they could and hope that their decisions were wise. Understandably, early survey research sometimes produced inaccurate results.

One of the most famous cases of a prediction based on inaccurate survey results involved the 1936 U.S. presidential election in which Franklin Roosevelt defeated Alf Landon. The magazine *Literary Digest* used its subscriber list along

A 19th Century Questionnaire for Investigating Child Development

Early psychologists developed questionnaires to address their research questions. The format and style of these questionnaires differed from the questionnaires that people encounter today. The items below come from a longer questionnaire that Théodore Simon developed in France to study child development.

Parents would complete this questionnaire and return it to the psychologist conducting the research. The psychologist would then tabulate the data to investigate patterns of development. The use of questionnaires to assess attitude and opinion followed the development of this type of instrument. Since that time, development of survey techniques has become much more sophisticated.

TABLE 4.1
Questionnaire for Studying Child Development

Topic	Item (Age of Child at Assessment)
Sight	Does the child's look indicate a vague contemplation (First day of life)
Hearing	Does the child searching for the one [i.e., the person] calling it? (Third month)
Recognition	Does it examine (with the lips pressed together) the object just being grasped? (Ninth and tenth month)
Motor Activities	Can it sit without any assistance? (Eleventh month)
Language	Where is little sister's (or mama's) hair? (Eighteen months to two years)

Source: Reymert, M. D. [No Year Specified.] Questionnaire for the observation of a young child from birth to two years of age. *Pedagogical Seminary*: 200–204.

with lists of automobile registrations and telephone users. The magazine sent 10 million questionnaires to people on these lists and received over two million replies. Based on the results of the survey, *Literary Digest* predicted that Landon would win with 57 percent of the vote. But the election results showed that having a large sample size for a survey does not guarantee valid data—Roosevelt won with 62 percent of the vote.

The problem that the magazine faced was sampling bias. When the survey was conducted, the United States was in the depths of the Great Depression. Only relatively wealthy people could afford magazine subscriptions, automobiles, and telephones, and this group tended to vote for Republican candidates. Poorer people, who tended to vote for Democrats, were largely missing from the sample.

In contrast to the massive, but invalid, sample contacted by the *Literary Digest*, a relatively unknown pollster named George Gallup predicted the outcome of the election within one percent. His sample included 50,000 respondents, much smaller than the magazine sample, but much more representative of the U.S. population. Today, Gallup polls are still widely used. The episode with the 1936 election is seen as the impetus for scientific polling that is common today.

Notwithstanding the *Literary Digest's* invalid prediction about the 1936 election, another well known mistake by pollsters occurred in the 1948 presidential election. Candidate Thomas Dewey held what appeared to be an insurmountable lead over candidate Harry Truman in the polls through the summer before the election. Because pollsters believed that voters had made up their minds as of two weeks prior to the election, they stopped surveying the electorate and missed the change in sentiment among voters. Harry Truman won the election. Clearly, the theory and methodology of survey research still required refinement.

Today, political polls are generally highly accurate, although the farther in advance of an election the polls are conducted, the greater the discrepancy between poll results and actual election results is likely to be. Voters may change their minds about which candidate to support and even about whether they will vote. So political polls may not be a good barometer of future voter behavior. When voters are sampled upon leaving a polling place, however, the results generally reflect the actual results quite accurately.

Psychologists and other behavioral scientists now study many different topics by means of survey research. One notable example is the General Social Survey (GSS), which was discussed in Chapter 3 and has been administered on a nearly annual basis since 1972 as a means of helping social scientists learn about American society. The GSS asks questions about many different topics ranging from A (Abortion) to Z (Zodiac), some related to significant social concerns and others related to a wide spectrum of generic issues and even popular culture.

Harry Truman celebrates his victory over Thomas Dewey in the 1948 U.S. presidential election. Early pollsters had not refined survey techniques, leading to the error in predicting the outcome of the election. *(Library of Congress)*

Respondents are randomly sampled from the population so the responses of the sample group are likely to be representative of the public in general.

THE NATURE OF ITEMS ON QUESTIONNAIRES
Format
Items on a questionnaire can take on different structures, but it is helpful to classify them according to the nature of the response they require. One format involves **open-ended questions** that allow respondents to provide whatever

answers they care to. For this type of question, an answer can go in many different directions because the person responding is free to interpret the meaning of the question and generate an answer that is unique to him or her. Other surveys utilize **closed-ended questions** that provide a list of acceptable answers; the respondent has to choose a response from the set provided. For many years, researchers thought that closed-ended items led to results with greater reliability and validity. The important issue revolved on categorizing responses.

Most questionnaires still tend to rely on closed-ended items because it is easier to tabulate the data when there is a limited range of responses. A common format is to provide a scale with a certain number of points from which a respondent must chooses one. A typical question might be "How easy or difficult is it for you to speak in front of a large audience?" where answer 1 would be *very easy*, answer 10 would be *very difficult*, and numbers between the two extremes would show different degrees of ease or difficulty.

The answer to this question is straightforward. It is a single number within a range from 1 to 10, and there is no wrong answer. On the other hand, if the question were open-ended and asked "Tell me how easy or difficult it is for you to speak in front of a large audience," respondents' answer would be less clearcut. For one thing, answers might be brief or long or even conditional (i.e., easy in certain circumstances and difficult in other circumstances). A person trying to categorize such a response would have a hard time categorizing it on a continuum ranging from easy to hard. If two people were categorizing the response separately, each might draw a different conclusion, raising the problem of data inconsistency.

Nonetheless, survey researchers now know that open-ended items can be as reliable and valid as closed-ended items, depending of course on how they are

The General Social Survey

People often talk about the "good old days." One aspect of life that was different in past decades was the belief that you can trust people. According to the data from the General Social Survey (GSS), trust in others has declined over the past three or four decades. In data like these, people very often believe that they can trust people who live around them or with whom they interact. But there is often a parallel belief that people living elsewhere are not trustworthy.

This type of question has appeared regularly on the GSS. It is important to recognize that this is an attitude question. It gives information on the degree to which people have faith in others, not whether people really have become less trustworthy than in the past.

interpreted and categorized. Since the 1940s, however, most investigators have used closed-ended questions most of the time. There are trade-offs in using one type of question or the other. Open-ended items may be easier to create than closed-ended items, but they are harder to code reliably. Closed-ended items are easier to score reliably, but there is a limited range of responses for the person completing the questionnaire to choose from, so the person may select a more or less acceptable answer, even if it isn't a personally precise answer.

Question Content

Most survey questions fall into three content-specific categories: memory questions, attitude or opinion questions, and demographic questions. With each of these come associated risks involving structure and wording. The greatest challenge is creating questions that are neutrally worded and that do not channel a respondent toward a particular answer. If you are conducting scientific research to find out what people think, the wording of your questions should permit respondents to answer accurately, not in a way that is influenced by the structure of wording of the item.

Memory Questions

There are four issues of concern with respect to memory questions. First, people may use different strategies in recalling events from the recent past than from the more distant past. Research has revealed that if people recall irritating events from the recent past, they focus on minor issues. If they recall such events from a more distant past, they tend to think of major events. Moreover, people are more likely to remember small detail and minor events that have just taken place, but those details may well have disappear over time.

Another concern with memory involves a phenomenon called **telescoping**. When you look through a telescope, distant objects appear close. In memory, the same phenomenon occurs—distant (in time) events seem close. So if an investigator wanted to know how long ago a person began to experience symptoms of depression, the person might report that the onset on such symptoms was somewhat recent even though the symptoms first surfaced some time ago.

A third difficulty associated with memory questions is that sometimes an item that appears at the beginning of a questionnaire might affect the response to a later question. Specifically, people want to appear consistent, so they might respond to a new question that relates to a previous question in a way that is consistent with the previous answer, even if that is not the best answer. Finally, on a particular closed-ended question, the scale of allowed answers may influence the response. When researchers asked respondents to indicate how many hours of television they watched each day, the answers differed depending on the lowest allowable answer on the scale, 0 to .5 hours versus 2.5 to 3 hours. It appears that when the scale began with 0 hours, respondents concluded that people generally tended to watch less television; if a scale began with 2.5 hours, respondents concluded that people watched more television. If respondents thought they were typical (or wanted to be perceived as typical), the low-scale group would select a smaller number, whereas the high-scale group would select a larger number, even if the television viewing habits of the two groups were relatively similar.

One other problem with memories is that they do not exist as independent entities. People often remember fragments of an event and fill in the gaps with plausible details. Or they may confuse two different events and merge them into one memory. When people answer memory questions in survey research, they may attempt to answer truthfully, but their memories may simply be erroneous. If you ask questions about memory that are too specific, people may be inclined to give their best guess, even if they do not remember an event very well or very accurately. On the other hand, if you ask questions that are too broad or vague, you may not get much useful information. Psychologists have developed techniques that allow them to obtain information that is valid, but memory accuracy remains a matter of concern.

Attitude Questions

Psychologists frequently survey people's attitudes about a wide variety of issues. The first attitude surveys in the PsycINFO database involved attitudes and beliefs about life after death. Since then, psychologists have used survey research to discover people's attitudes on a wide variety of issues. Attitude questions pose some of the same structural concerns as memory questions, but there are several issues that are more relevant for the measurement of attitudes than the measurement of memory.

Just as the wording of a question can affect responses about memory, it can affect responses about attitude. Researchers have found, for example, that people are more inclined to support "assistance to the poor" than they are to support "welfare." If two different researchers asked for the same information but one referred to "assistance to the poor" and the other referred to "welfare," the results would likely lead to very different impressions regarding support for potential social policy involving people living in poverty. Researchers must therefore attend to the wording of questionnaire items very carefully, avoiding language and phrasing that can prompt a response to language rather than the topic they are being asked about. One subtle factor that influences how people respond might simply be their perception of the purpose of a questionnaire. In one study, researchers gave respondents one of two versions of the same a survey; the question were identical, but the wording at the top of the two versions was different. On one version, the heading was "Institute for Personality Research"; on the other, it was "Institute for Social Research." People who believed that they were responding to a socially oriented survey focused on social issues; people who believed that they were responding to a personality survey focused on personality.

Another issue associated with attitude research is how to deal with sensitive or controversial topics. People may simply be reluctant to share their attitudes on topics like abortion, legalization of marijuana, or racial issues. If respondents understand that their answers will be anonymous and confidential, they may be more likely to give honest answers, but this is no guarantee that their answers will be honest. In some instances, the response to a sensitive question is no response whatsoever.

Another concern in attitude research is that there is no accurate way to gauge whether people actually have an attitude or opinion about a given topic or, if they do, how deeply they feel about it. Here researchers are somewhat curiously hindered by respondent cooperation. What this means is that if respondents believe that a researcher is asking a legitimate question (and researchers do ask legitimate questions just about 100 percent of the time), they try to come up with a reasonable response. Most respondents recognize that their purpose is not to lie or to deceive the researcher but to be helpful participants in research. The problem arises when the intention to be helpful interferes with the true purpose of the research.

To test this concept, investigators have created questions about fictional issues (e.g., the amount of aid that the government should send to a nonexistent country) and queried people on their attitudes about these issues. Respondents could not have had a preexisting attitude about any of the issues because the researchers invented them, but this did not stop them from expressing an attitude. It is not clear how prevalent this type of response is, but because such answers do not represent a real attitude, they compromises the quality of the data.

Researchers also recognize that somebody might have an well-defined attitude on a real topic, but the person may or may not hold that attitude deeply. So a person might favor laws that ban driving an automobile while sending a text message or using a laptop computer, but that same individual may not hold the attitude deeply enough to write a letter to a legislator expressing an opinion. As such, a large percentage of the population might be in favor of or in opposition to some issue, but they may not feel strongly enough to do anything about it.

RESPONSE BIASES

Generally, respondents try to be helpful to researchers by providing information that is both informative and accurate. Sometimes, however, people completing a survey (or any other task for that matter) do not always provide the best answer to a question because of **response biases**, patterns of responding that do not reflect a person's real memories or attitudes. People who have low motivation, who are less well educated, or who face questions requiring complex thought, sometimes engage in **satisficing,** providing the first answer they think of that is acceptable, even if it is not the best answer. The complement to satisficing is **optimizing**, a process that involves searching for the best answer to a question, even if it is hard to come up that answer.

Another issue that surfaces with memory questions is that people try to provide as much detail as they confidently can. At some point, however, there is a limit to detail that can be remembered; anything beyond this point would involve making up details that are plausible but in which the respondent has decreasing confidence. The answer can be affected depending on the criterion the person sets for providing an answer he or she thinks is appropriate.

The recognition that survey format sometimes influences responses is important and has prompted some changes in how surveys are conducted. Each new format, however, raises its own difficulties. Over the past half century, for example, telephone surveys have replaced face-to-face interviews because telephone surveys are easier, cheaper, and quicker. One problem that psychologist Jon Krosnick has identified with such surveys is that people surveyed by phone tend to satisfice, to be uncooperative with the surveyor, are suspicious about the survey, show elevated levels of social desirability bias, and resent the length of time that more extended surveys take (even though such surveys invariably

Are People Sicker by Mail than Over the Phone?

When surveyed about their health, people tend to respond differently to different survey delivery modes. They typically give answers that suggest better health when the survey is conducted by telephone and worse health when the survey is conducted by mail. A group of researchers led by Noel Brewer investigated the question of why this might occur. They contacted and queried 719 war veterans from the United States about their health status. Some veterans received phone calls; others received letters in the mail.

The researchers discovered that mailed surveys resulted in greater numbers of medical symptoms than phone surveys. The reason seems to be that respondents faced a relatively complex cognitive task in listing symptoms while the surveyor was on the phone. The task was simpler when they were completing the survey on paper. On the phone, respondents tended to omit mild (and, to a lesser degree, moderate symptoms); on paper, such symptoms were included.

The investigators concluded that the veterans were satisficing while answering on the phone. Fortunately, when the researchers controlled for the omission of the mild symptoms, they discovered that the symptoms that the veterans did report were useful in establishing how well they were able to function.

take less time than a face-to-face survey). Mail surveys come with their own set of problems. The previous sidebar shows how survey format can affect a respondent's answers and, by extension, a researcher's conclusions.

Another source of bias in responses is **acquiescence**, the tendency to agree with an item on a questionnaire regardless of the content of the item. The lower the educational level, intelligence, and age, the higher the likelihood that respondents will resort to acquiescence. This correlation has prompted researchers to question whether research results conducted with college students, the most widely surveyed population, will represent people in general. Taking into account the tendency to acquiesce, they have discovered that responses by the college population seem to match those of a more general sample, at least with respect to personality measurement.

One common bias is a tendency to answer questions in a predictable way, regardless of the content of those questions. Some people, for example, show a preference for responding "yes" if given a choice between yes and no. Or they may show a tendency to rate somebody or something in the middle of a scale, generally avoiding extremes. Obviously, such responses are not helpful to researchers except to confirm that this bias exists.

Another type of response bias can occur when people answer questions about their own personal characteristics. Just as people in everyday social situations want others to evaluate them positively, people who complete questionnaires want to be seen in a good light and respond to questions in a way that portrays them positively. The response bias associated with generating a positive impression of oneself is called **social desirability bias**. Until recently, this bias was seen as having two manifestations. One is called **impression management** and involves a conscious attempt by the respondent to deceive the researcher; the person gives responses that he or she knows are inaccurate.

A second variation of social desirability bias does not involve active deception. Those engaging in this form of bias are attempting to give valid and honest responses. They provide answers that are generally accurate, but they have a rosier picture of themselves and provide answers that are more positive than objectively warranted. This bias is called **self-deception positivity**.

Social desirability bias has received scrutiny with regard to gender differences in responses. Researchers Walter Vispoel and Ellen Forte Fast observed that male and female respondents report different levels of competence in mathematics, reinforcing the stereotype that men are better at math than women are. Interestingly, when the researchers attempted to verify the gender differences, they found that the stereotype did not hold up. These psychologists concluded that the respondents were showing impression management prompted by the desire to make their behavior consistent with the stereotype. Other investigators have found social desirability bias in research in such varied areas as self-concept, sexual behavior, and attendance at religious services.

Would You Continue to Work If You Were Rich?

People complain that the work ethic of Americans is not as strong as it used to be, indicating a belief that in the past, people viewed work as important for its own sake. Figure 4.1 below, based on over 20,000 people interviewed between 1972 and 2008, shows how people's responses to a related question have fluctuated over the years. There are many possible reasons for the pattern of responses. Some research suggests that a social desirability bias is at work. People who feel the need to be seen favorably were more likely to say that they would continue to work than those with less of that particular need. In addition, when economic times are hard, people are more likely to say that they would continue to work.

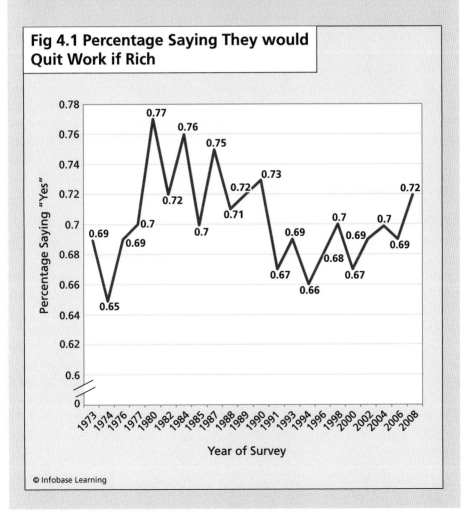

Fig 4.1 Percentage Saying They would Quit Work if Rich

© Infobase Learning

More recent research has focused on gender differences in the context of answers. In this newer view, one dimension of bias is related to what psychologists call *agency*, which is related to such characteristics as dominance, assertiveness, control, mastery and similar characteristics. The second dimension has to do with *communion*, which is related to characteristics like affiliation, nurturance, approval, connectedness. It appears that there indeed is a gender difference in the type of social desirability bias that male and female respondents display. Response biases by women are more likely to be associated with communal characteristics, whereas men lean in the direction of bias associated with agency.

Psychologists continue to study response bias both because of its importance to survey research and because of its complexity. There is some evidence that particular personality traits are associated with various types of social desirability bias and that there may be national trends associated with the dimensions of collectivism and individualism, but the picture is still far from clear. One of the reasons that we still have a lot to learn about people's response patterns is that most research on the topic of social desirability has involved college students in the United States. Some research with international samples led by E. M. Jan-Benedict shows similarities in the results from the student samples, but subtle differences across samples may be important. One example of how social desirability bias may influence responses involves the question of whether people would continue to work if they won the lottery. The GSS has regularly asked respondents if they would continue to work if they were rich. The results of such surveys over the years have been quite telling.

SELECTING RESPONDENTS

In theory, it would be a good idea to question everybody in your population of interest when conducting survey research, but that is often unrealistic. For instance, for a nationwide political poll in the United States, there may be 100 million potential voters. If a surveyor took one minute to survey each potential voter, it would take that surveyor about 190 years to complete the research. The candidates' great-great grandchildren might be running for office at that time.

So the strategy that polling organizations use is to select a sample of respondents that will be representative of the whole population. The statistics are complicated, but pollsters are generally satisfied with a well-chosen sample of about 1,000 people. How well does this strategy work? Generally, it works pretty well. There are occasional problems with samples, but the professionals know how to create a **sampling frame**, the subset of the population from which they draw the sample.

At the same time, there are several possible reasons for inaccuracy in such polls. For example, people may change their minds between the day they respond to the poll and election day. Some may be reluctant to state their true opinion or may simply refuse to answer. Sometimes, a poll may be well designed, but results in a sample that does not reflect the population through simple bad luck.

Another issue that affects predicting the outcome of an election is how close the race is. Tight races are harder to call accurately because a slight change in the makeup of a sample can lead to a small degree of error in the prediction and thus affect the broader conclusions of the pollsters. Nonetheless, after over half a century of experience and research on survey techniques, the pollsters have well-established and effective methodologies.

Sampling Strategies

The ideal approach for pollsters who want a sample that mirrors the population is to use **probability sampling**. This approach involves identifying the population precisely and then selecting on some random basis a specified number of people. Although it may be counterintuitive to some, random sampling is a very useful strategy because it generally avoids samples with a built-in bias.

Techniques can get complicated, but the most basic approach is **simple random sampling** in which the entire population is identified, then names are selected randomly. Sometimes researchers want to make sure that certain types of people are represented in the sample in the proportions that the researchers deem appropriate. Such a strategy is called **stratified random sampling**.

For example, in research by Hyun-Sil Kim and Hun-Soo Kim on family dynamics and their relation to juvenile delinquency in Korea, the investigators used stratified random sampling to generate a sample of adolescents either in school or in a juvenile correctional facility. They created a sample of 2,100 adolescents with specific proportions of adolescents in middle school, high school, and correctional facilities; they also balanced their sample to include urban and rural respondents. In the end, the investigators were confident that their sample mirrored the population and that they could generalize their findings from this sample. The results revealed that there were significantly greater problems with family dynamics and violence in the families of juvenile delinquents, who also showed higher levels of psychological problems.

Most psychological research does not involve probability samples. Rather, psychologists typically makes use of **nonprobability sampling**. These samples may not include a balance of different types of respondents that are representative of the broader population. One term used to describe most psychological samples is **convenience samples**—samples, as the name implies, that are easy and convenient for the researcher to obtain. Most such research recruits college students as respondents. This begs the question whether such samples mirror the entire population. Depending on the questions asked and the particulars of the sample, the student responses may resemble those of the population, but it would be generally unwise to assume that the students constitute a representative sample.

There are other variations within probability and nonprobability sampling, but what all of the probabilistic techniques have in common is a high likelihood that the selected sample will represent the population. In contrast, it is quite doubtful that this will be the case with convenience samples. But the advantage of using convenience samples lies in economy (both in terms of time and in terms of money), which is why many researchers use such samples.

Further Reading

Beins, Bernard C. *Research Methods: A Tool for Life*. Boston, MA US: Pearson, 2009.

CHAPTER 5

ETHICS IN RESEARCH

In an ideal world, scientists would simply develop research questions, create the methodology to answer those questions, conduct a study, and draw conclusions based on the data. However, we do not live in an ideal world, so there is an extra step that investigators are required to take before they can carry out a study. That step involves protecting the people or animals who take part in the study. Ethical issues are important not only for moral reasons but also for legal reasons. Laws exist for the protection of participants in research.

Most scientists are undoubtedly as ethical and caring of others as anybody else. Sometimes, though, researchers have engaged in projects that endangered research participants. In some instances, the researchers were aware of the problems they caused, like the Nazi doctors in World War II who conducted cruel experiments on human victims or the American doctors who knowingly fed radioactive substances to developmentally disabled children to learn about the body's absorption of minerals. In most other cases in which ethical lapses have been identified, researchers may simply have overlooked the potential for harm to study participants. The harm in such cases might be physical (e.g., muscle aches in a study on physical endurance) or it might be psychological (e.g., embarrassment in a study about self-esteem).

When psychologists (and all other scientists studying human and many nonhuman animals) plan studies, they must submit a plan to an **Institutional Review Board** (IRB), and this plan must outline any potential risks to participants. In the behavioral sciences, the risks are generally minimal, but researchers must still follow the laws governing human-related research.

The IRB's function is to ensure that the potential risks do not outweigh the benefits of the research. If the potential risks are deemed too great, the researchers are denied permission to conduct the study. If there are lesser potential risks, investigators may be able to conduct their study as long as they provide a plan on how they will successfully deal with any problems that might arise.

It is important to keep in mind that any potential risk is just that—potential. That is, neither the researchers nor the IRB can know if such potential problems will occur and not all potential problems can be anticipated. Thus, despite precautions, participants in a given study might suffer some harm. The best that the researchers can do is to give careful consideration to the possibilities and do their best to develop a plan that will help them deal with problems. As noted above, we do not live in an ideal world, so we need to reach decisions based on the best information we have. Fortunately, psychological research seldom results in harm, trouble, or even inconvenience for participants.

HOW RESEARCHERS APPROACH ETHICAL ISSUES

The first principle of ethics in research is to safeguard participants who volunteer to be studied. The two components of risk include the possibility that a participant will suffer either physical harm or psychological harm. When scientists evaluate risk issues, they consider short-term and long-term problems. In psychological research, there is generally not much possibility of physical harm to participants, either short or long term. If any risk exists, it tends to be psychological and probably short-term. For instance, if a person in a research study is deceived, he or she might be embarrassed; this would constitute potential psychological harm. It may be short lived, but the researcher needs to take it into account and to make sure that the person leaves the experimental session in a positive psychological state.

When researchers consider the details of how to protect participants, they need to pay attention to the specifics of the research and the social context in which the research occurs. The guidelines are fairly simple, but applying them involves considering some complicated issues. The principles developed by the U.S. government regarding treatment of participants appear in the sidebar that accompanies this section. These guidelines resemble an internationally adopted set of principles, the Nuremburg Code that was developed as a result of Nazi atrocities during World War II.

Some examples of how researchers think about risk issues are cited below. Some of the concerns are rather obvious, but others are more subtle. Ethical researchers take all of these issues seriously. Note that all of these issues exemplify most of the U.S. government's principles for ethical research: the question of informed consent, maximizing the results of the research while minimizing

General Principles in Treating Human Subjects

The U. S. government created a commission that developed a set of fundamental ethical principles that researchers studying human participants must follow. These principles were compiled in the Belmont Report (named for the conference center at which they were developed).

Respect for persons: protecting the autonomy of all people and treating them with courtesy and respect and allowing for informed consent;

Beneficence: maximizing benefits for the research project while minimizing risks to the research subjects; and

Justice: ensuring reasonable, non-exploitative, and well-considered procedures are administered fairly (the fair distribution of costs and benefits to potential research participants.)

Fidelity: fairness and equality.

Non-maleficence: Do no harm.

Veracity: Be truthful, no deception.

risk to participants, not exploiting participants, avoiding harm, and avoiding deception. These principles take different forms depending on the nature of a given research program.

Although these principles seem obvious and straightforward, researchers of the past did not always conduct research that reflected the ethical standards they embody. Half a century ago, for example, researchers conducted experiments with hallucinogenic drugs (e.g., LSD). It was only because of political and social forces that such research stopped. More recently, a new generation of investigators has once again developed research programs with such drugs. Some of the questions they are asking involve the degree to which these drugs generate the same responses in the brain that psychotic episodes do or whether these drugs can alleviate some of the symptoms of depression and anxiety that people with terminal cancer experience.

What are the potential risks for such research? In general, the hallucinogens used in these experiments are not physiologically addictive, nor do they lead to other physical problems. Moreover, and perhaps surprisingly, the potential risk of physical harm under controlled conditions is fairly small and are limited to minor side-effects like dizziness, muscle weakness, slightly elevated blood pressure, or dilated pupils. Although the use of hallucinogens in unsupervised and uncontrolled conditions could lead to physical harm to users, in a controlled, laboratory situation, the risk of physical harm is low. There is a greater potential for psychological side-effects as some people may experience responses like anxiety, paranoia, frightening illusions, or troubling thoughts. Consequently, problems in research with hallucinogens manifest themselves primarily among people who are psychologically troubled to begin with. As participants in experiments with hallucinogens, some of these individuals have experienced psychotic-like symptoms that lasted for a day or two. In general, however, extreme reactions are rare even in such populations and are virtually nonexistent among people without a diagnosed psychological disorder. The ethical objectives related to such experiments are fairly straightforward and have been seriously addressed by psychologists. Researchers led by M.W. Johnson, for example, have suggested that research with hallucinogens can be conducted ethically if the researchers are fastidious in selecting participants who are physically and psychological healthy, if they are knowledgeable about adverse reactions and qualified to deal with them, and if they create a safe and accommodating research environment that meets a high level of ethical standards.

Another ethical issue deals with the question of whether participants know that they are in a research study and whether subjects are competent to decide if they want to participate. Government standards deriving from the Belmont Report now mandate that all participants in psychological research studies must be advised about purpose and nature of a study, to the extent that they know enough about the study to make an informed decision about participation.

One example that illustrates this concept of informed consent centers on research practices of certain tobacco companies. A group of researchers led by Patricia McDaniel studied records of research tobacco companies conducted to determine how cigarettes taste when the tobacco used in them was grown by farmers who used two particular pesticides. The participants in this research were employees of the tobacco companies who were told only that the company wanted them to "evaluate the cigarettes." From this loose description, it is difficult to gauge whether it was entirely clear to workers that they were participating in research. In addition, it is not clear whether participate was voluntary or mandatory (i.e., whether workers felt their jobs might be in jeopardy if they did not participate). Given these ambiguities, there may have been inadequate informed consent and participation may not have been truly voluntary.

Because they fund their own research, tobacco companies are not legally mandated to create institutional review boards (some companies do so voluntarily; others do not). Thus, the research ethics applied may be strict or loose in relation to those enumerated in the Belmont Report. The companies involved in the McDaniel study did have an IRB, but because members of the IRB were company employees, they would have had a vested interest in having the research completed, raising the clear potential for conflict of interest.

This example provides a picture of the *possible* ethical problems that can arise in research situations, but it is important to note that records from the past are created for a particular purpose and that subsequent researchers use them for a different purpose. The McDaniel study is a case in point. Because our knowledge about the tobacco-related research is so limited, we cannot assume that the companies were remiss in their duty to protect participants.

These research examples in this section illustrate some of the ethical issues that can arise in research and raise a number of important research considerations, some hypothetical and some real. Other issues examined in this chapter will be discussed in the context of research that is specifically known for the ethical concerns that it posed.

HISTORICAL PROBLEMS

There have been several notable research programs that have generated discussion about unethical practices. In some cases, the research was potentially legitimate, but the investigators showed little consideration for participants to the extent that the research caused great harm and even led to the death of participants. The examples described in this section highlight problems within the research continuum, ranging from research with essentially no ethical implications to research with extreme and severe ethical implications.

The studies here are more oriented to biomedical research than psychological research, but the ethical issues are the same as those that psychologists engaged in research must consider. The research programs described here would not take place today because of the legal safeguards that have been created to minimize the possibility that research participants will suffer either physical or psychological harm.

The Tuskegee Syphilis Study

One infamous research program plagued by severe ethical problems was a decades-long study on the effects of untreated syphilis. The study took place during the 1930s and subject participants were poor, black men in Tuskegee, Alabama, all infected with syphilis. The first major breach of ethics was the failure of the doctors involved in the study to inform the subjects of the nature of the study, thus precluding informed consent. An even more serious breach of ethics was the subsequent failure to treat the infected men, even when effective medication became available.

Some have argued that the study was initially ethically neutral because the investigators were supposedly studying the progression of a disease for which there was no effective treatment at the time. The only substances used to treat syphilis in the 1930s were, at best, only mildly effective; others were quite toxic themselves. Today, however, most scientists would agree that ethical problems increased exponentially as the study continued.

Researchers first identified the population who would be the subjects in the study—the poor, black men infected with syphilis. The plan was to study these men for six to nine months to see the progression of the disease, then to treat them. As it turned out, the subjects were never treated for the disease and the study continued for 40 years until a Public Health Service professional, Dr. Peter Buxtun, revealed what was occurring to the *Washington Post* in 1972.

The first significant problem with this study was a clear violation of the principle of **informed consent**. The men believed that they were being treated for so-called "bad blood," a term that was widely used as a catch-all term for several maladies. They did not know they were part of a research study on syphilis. Today, the law mandates that people be given enough information to enable an informed decision about whether they will participate in any given research. But in 1932, when the study began, there was no such requirement.

A second important problem with this study was that participation in the study was not voluntary. For one thing, the men did not know that they were research subjects in a study on syphilis, so they could not have been considered "volunteers." In addition, they were promised free health care for minor problems, free transportation to the clinic, and free meals on days they were at the clinic. In return, they underwent a painful spinal tap and agreed to be autopsied after their deaths. Furthermore, most of the men were sharecroppers and were encouraged by the land owners on whose lands they worked to participate in the study—a situation that strongly suggests the men felt they really did not have a choice and had to participate or risk losing their livelihood.

Today, researchers are forbidden to offer large monetary (or other) inducements to prospective study participants, especially to poor people who might find the inducements so enticing that they agree to participate even in high-risk studies. In this respect, such offers are now considered essentially coercive.

Another major ethical lapse of the Tuskegee study involved the failure of the researchers to treat their syphilitic subjects with penicillin, which became available in the late 1940s and might have cured them. The investigators kept the study running for a quarter of a century after effective treatment was developed and actively prevented the men from receiving appropriate medical care.

The impact of this research has continued well beyond its termination in 1972. Because of the Tuskegee study, many black Americans do not trust the government or the Public Health Service. Decades after the study ended, there is evidence that this population may not seek preventive health care for fear of being victimized in a similar way.

Radiation Studies

Another set of studies that were ethically troublesome took place in conjunction with the Massachusetts Institute of Technology and the Walter E. Fernald State School (now called the Walter E. Fernald Developmental Center). The residential school housed children who were diagnosed as developmentally disabled, although some estimates suggest that many children had IQ scores that fell within the "normal" range.

The Fernald studies posed several significant ethical problems. The issue of informed consent is especially troublesome in this case. Some populations are more vulnerable than others, and children clearly fall within this group. This vulnerability is even more pronounced in the case of children with developmental disabilities. Clearly, such children are not likely to understand much about research studies or what they risk by participating in such studies. As such, the right to agree to participation is generally accorded to the parents. But in the Fernald research, the parents making decisions for their developmentally disabled children were told that the children were going to participate in nutrition research, a clear-cut matter of deception. They were, in fact, informed by letter that research the had the purpose "of helping to improve the nutrition of our children and to help them in general more efficiently than before."

In reality, the purpose of the research was not to benefit the children through improved nutrition but to benefit the researchers by providing them with an opportunity to learn about the body's absorption of iron and calcium. In addition, the research involved adding radioactive isotopes to food that was then given to the children—a fact that was not revealed to their parents. Scientists have subsequently concluded that the level of exposure to radioactivity was so small that it was likely that there was no physical harm (either immediately or long term) from the radiation. The fact remains that those legally empowered to give informed consent on behalf of their children were not informed but deceived.

Inducement was also a problem. Researchers told parents that the children, who were members of a science club, would get a quart of milk daily, go to a baseball game and the beach, and occasionally have dinners outside the school. Because conditions at the school were so poor (there were up to 36 boys in a single dormitory room, and the facilities were in disrepair, there were reports of abuse), the proffered inducement was well nigh irresistible.

As a sequel to this discussion, it must be noted that this was not the only research study involving radioactive substances. There have, in fact, been numerous studies at various laboratories across the country that have made use of radioactive iodine, uranium, plutonium, and radium. In many instances, the issue of voluntary, informed participation seems to have been disregarded altogether.

Behavioral Research on Stuttering

Another troubling study took place in a residential facility for children during the Great Depression. Focused on behavioral principles, the study was conducted by a woman named Mary Tudor, later known as The Monster; because of her, the study itself became known as "The Monster Study." The major ethical issues raised by this study include the use of a vulnerable group (children), the problem of long-term physical and psychological harm; and **compensatory**

follow-up (the process of contacting participants after potentially risky studies to see if there are any long-term negative consequences).

This study is especially interesting to psychologists because of its complexity and because it clearly raises the conundrum of holding researchers from the past accountable by today's ethical standards. Some research falls easily into this paradigm because it is so heinous that people of every historical era would see it as unconscionable. Examples include withholding and preventing treatment for the syphilis-infected men in the Tuskegee study and the horrific experiments conducted by Nazi doctors during World War II. But other research cannot be so easily classified, partly because it may be somewhat understandable (if not excusable) if viewed from the perspective of historical context and especially from the perspective of people living in a certain time and place within that context. The case of Mary Tudor and the ethics of the so-called monster study are a good deal murkier when we consider the research from the viewpoint that somebody from that era would have had.

Essentially, the research was to study the emergence of stuttering. It was supposed to involve four groups of children who lived in a residential facility in Iowa. Table 5.1 shows how Tudor laid out the study.

As the table shows, Tudor planned to induce stuttering in two groups of children and reduce stuttering in two other groups. The overarching question here is why she would plan and carry out this study at all. The answer must be addressed in the context of the 1930s, a time when social researchers were generally behaviorists, who believed that any given behavior arose due to reinforce-

TABLE 5.1
Design of the so-called
"Monster Study" conducted by Mary Tudor

	Stutterers	Nonstutterers
Induce Stuttering	The researcher would call attention to stuttering behavior among children who had a stuttering problem, reinforcing it to see if it increased.	The researcher would call attention to stuttering behavior among children who had normal speech, reinforcing it to see if it increased.
Reduce Stuttering	The researcher would tell stuttering children that their speech was normal, reinforcing normal speech to see if it increased.	The researcher would tell nonstuttering children that their speech was normal, reinforcing normal speech to see if it persisted.

ment and was extinguished by nonreinforcement. Speech disorder researchers believed that these principles were applicable to inducing and extinguishing stuttering. So it would be reasonable, according to behavioral theory, to conduct tests to see if stuttering could be induced and extinguished through reinforcement principles. That is exactly what Mary Tudor seemed to have in mind. According to modern theory and social awareness, no IRB would ever approve such research today. But there were no IRBs back then. Besides, researchers believed in the power of behavioral theory, and by extension, believed that they would be doing no lasting harm to the children they studied because if they could condition stuttering, they could also eliminate it. So, as strange as the research seems from today's theoretical perspective, you could argue that it would not do damage to the children and that the knowledge it provided would ultimately be beneficial for stutterers.

The research gained prominence in 2001 when a reporter for the *San Jose Mercury News* wrote a story about it. Naturally, there was outrage that the research had been perpetrated on the children involved. But there is some ambiguity in this situation, too.

First of all, there is no doubt that the children, some of whom came from impoverished families, were exploited in ways that children from wealthier backgrounds would not have been; in the era during which the studies were conducted, if a family could not afford to raise a child, that child might be sent to an orphanage, and this was in fact the case for some of the children in Tudor's study. Back then, the practice of using such children in research studies was not seen as problematic. However we might judge the situation by today's standards, it is not clear that Tudor or her adviser, Wendell Johnson, thought that there was anything wrong with the practice.

A second important issue is whether Tudor and Johnson believed that the research would cause long-term damage to the children. If the dominant theory of the time was that the research would lead them to conclude that any induced stuttering could be extinguished, we might conclude that they acted in good faith. A third issue involves compensatory follow-up, a practice researchers use to make sure that they undo any problems they may have caused. Tudor seems to have tried to undo the stuttering, but researchers Nicoline Grinager Ambrose and Ehud Yairi pointed out that the research design of the project was flawed, even by the standards of those times, and that the research was entirely unsuccessful in changing speech patterns anyway. It is clear from Figure 5.1 that the change in speech fluency from the start to the end of the study was minimal; in three of the four groups, fluency actually improved, although not significantly. The single group that in which fluency declined involved children who were reinforced as having fluent speech.

So how do we evaluate the research in ethical terms? Clearly, from a modern perspective, the research was ethically untenable. There was no informed

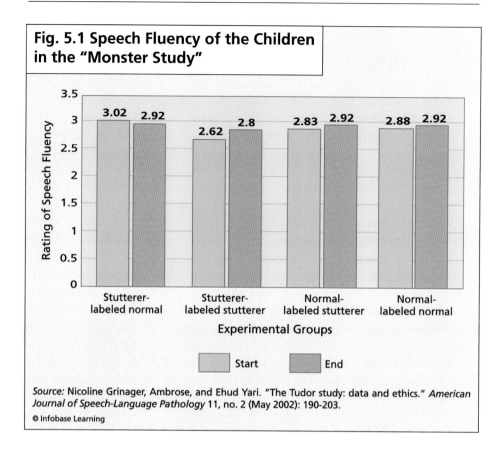

Fig. 5.1 Speech Fluency of the Children in the "Monster Study"

Source: Nicoline Grinager, Ambrose, and Ehud Yari. "The Tudor study: data and ethics." *American Journal of Speech-Language Pathology* 11, no. 2 (May 2002): 190-203.

© Infobase Learning

consent, the subjects were from a vulnerable population, the participation was not voluntary, there was risk of long-term damage, and there was no compensatory follow-up. From the perspective of the 1930s, however, one could not conclude unambiguously that Mary Tudor was not acting in good faith.

Stanley Milgram's Obedience Studies

The ethical questions associated with Milgram's studies of the 1960s are best understood in the social context in which they occurred. During the second world war, Nazi doctors performed cruel medical research on prisoners in concentration camps, conducting experiments that caused injury, extreme pain, and death. Concentration camp guards perpetrated other cruelty on victims. After the war, a number of those found guilty of committing these atrocities claimed that they were merely following orders.

This exculpatory response piqued Stanley Milgram's interest. He planned a series of studies to see the degree to which experimental subjects would obey orders that had the potential to cause death to another person in the study. Milgram's experiment was set up to make one group of participants think that they were engaging in activity that was dangerous and harmful to others. Nobody participating in the study was physically harmed.

One ethical question that arises immediately concerns Milgram's obvious and intentional deception in telling participants that they were taking part in

Obedience in Experimental Research

Stanley Milgram's obedience research involved collusion between Milgram, as the experimenter, and an actor who pretended that he was being subjected to electrical shocks of increasing intensity. Together they convinced a series of unwitting study participants to administer a shock to the actor (who was supposedly strapped to a chair in another room) each time the actor appeared to make a mistake in a learning task.

The strength of the shocks were to begin at 15 volts and continued to a level marked "Danger-XXX." At some point in the study, the actor, who had claimed to have a heart problem, would stop responding, giving the impression that he might be dead. About two-thirds of the participants administering the shocks continued to the highest shock level, although many of them showed signs of significant distress.

Milgram's ideas for this research may have had their origins in the work he performed with Solomon Asch on conformity. Milgram studied the degree to which people in a judgment task would conform with others who had made obviously incorrect judgments. Milgram studied such conformity among people in Norway and France in one of the first cross-national studies in psychology.

His decision to study obedience was further motivated by a desire to understand the systematic murder of Jews by the Nazis in the second world war. He decided to perform the first studies on Americans, certain that they would resist the experimenter's insistence on continuing. The second phase of the study would be conducted in Germany, where he anticipated that participants would blindly obey. As it turned out, Milgram did not need to conduct the studies in Germany because the American participants, contrary to his assumption, obeyed orders to escalate the intensity of the electric shocks, thus behaving in a manner that was both atypical and unanticipated.

Even in the 1960s, there was considerable criticism to Milgram's research; it is highly unlikely that such research would be approved by an IRB today. Recently, however, some investigators have attempted a modified replication if Milgram's research, using a methodology that would not be associated with significant risk issues.

a study on learning. In addition, critics claimed that he did not respect participants' well-being, subjected them to considerable psychological and physical harm (three participants experienced seizures), and failed to follow-up after the fact to ameliorate the harm done. There is also a question as to whether their participation was truly voluntary; during the study, those who wanted to stop were told that they had to continue. Though there were no physical restraints keeping them in their seats and no physical threat that forced them to continue, they might have continued solely as a result of the authoritative commands they were given, and thus their participation might be construed as marginally or not entirely voluntary.

Although these claims have some merit, it is important to understand the Milgram research in its social context. In addition, before a study actually begins, risks are only potential—that is, no one can know with any certainty whether actual harm will occur. These two points help us understand why the research was done as it was.

In terms of social context, Americans (and others) were still experiencing the after-effects of World War II. Furthermore, the country had recently entered a new kind of conflict—the early years of a cold war with Russia. There was widespread belief that communism turned people into human machines who would have no freedom. In short, people were quite worried about the future of the country. This concern might have prompted and condoned research that we might question or condemn today; it is likely in fact that researchers of the time (including Milgram) considered such experiments legitimate and appropriate, viewing any negative impact on participants as an acceptable price to pay for the knowledge we would gain about blind obedience to authority and how to avoid it.

In addition, Milgram did not go into the study haphazardly. To assess how likely participants would be to continue administering what they thought were extreme shocks, he asked a group of psychiatrists to estimate the percentage of participants who would give the extreme shocks. These experts thought that only a small percentage would do so. Consequently, Milgram was acting with the belief that he would not be putting people in a stressful situation because they would be unwilling to administer dangerous or lethal shocks and would therefore not suffer the stress of doing so. Unfortunately, the experts were very wrong. Neither they nor Milgram anticipated that the results would occur as they did.

After the experiments, Milgram met with participants and explained to them what the study was really about. The participants were also introduced to the actor who was supposedly being shocked and were able to see that he was perfectly fine and in good spirits. Milgram also engaged in compensatory follow-up, having a psychiatrist contact some participants after some time had elapsed to see that they were not experiencing negative consequences because of their participation. Subsequently, other researchers studied Milgram's debriefing protocol and discovered that it was successful in reducing tension in participants.

Milgram conducted numerous experiments to assess the expression of so-called destructive obedience, leaving a legacy that has spurred much discussion about obedience, research methodology, and ethics. After he conducted his research, Milgram applied for membership in the American Psychological Association. His acceptance was delayed while the APA evaluated his work to determine whether he had engaged in inappropriate or unethical behavior. After studying the situation, the APA concluded that Milgram had not violated ethical codes and awarded him membership.

On June 1, 1962, Milgram wrote a letter to the chair of the Psychology Department at Yale University (where he worked), stating that his obedience studies were completed. Psychologist Thomas Blass, an expert on Milgram and his work, pointed out the irony of the timing of this letter—it was written the day after Israel had executed Adolph Eichmann, who was instrumental in the murder of millions of Jews by the Nazis during WWII.

Psychologist Jerry Burger has replicated Milgram's research with a scaled-down, less stressful methodology that passed an IRB review. He found slightly lower obedience rates than Milgram did. Some people have noted that Burger's research did not lead to the same emotional distress in participants that Milgram's did. But it is highly unlikely (maybe impossible) that an IRB would approve a direct replication of Milgram's original research. Burger's research does show, however, that it is possible to study obedience in the laboratory and still respect the rights of participants.

In hindsight, Milgram's study answers some ethical questions and raises others. Participants in the study experienced distress at levels that Milgram (as well as the psychiatrists he consulted with) could not predict. He did engage in post-study debriefing sessions that seemed successful, and he provided compensatory follow-up for some participants to see if there were long-term problems. The APA, while concerned by his work, did not find it a reason to deny him membership in the organization. And other psychologists have deemed his work important enough to study and even replicate, with modification, of course. The ethical questions still remain; the answers are still not absolutely clear-cut.

Philip Zimbardo's Prison Study

In 1971 psychologist Philip Zimbardo set up a study at Stanford University involving college students who adopted the roles either of prisoners or prison guards in a simulated jail. According to the IRB application that Zimbardo submitted, he stated that he intended the study to last about one week, although the informed consent form stated that the duration would be one to two weeks. In fact, Zimbardo terminated the study after six days because the guards had become brutal toward the prisoners, and the prisoners were showing signs of significant stress.

The main ethical issues associated with this study were the significant distress that participants experienced and the apparent lack of voluntary participation once the study was underway. Today, participants must be told that they are free to withdraw from a study at any point without any penalty. In Zimbardo's application to conduct the research, he specifically stated that the participants would be discouraged from withdrawing.

These criticisms, like those regarding Milgram's research, would be entirely valid according to the ethical standards that researchers use today. But the guidelines were different at the time the research took place. So although it is clear that the Zimbardo study would not receive approval today; one can make a defensible argument (with which some people would disagree) that the study was not unethical at that time.

DECEPTION RESEARCH

Deception has been a part of psychological research for decades, but any investigator who uses deception must consider the ethics of lying to participants about some aspect of a study. Deception in research can be active or passive. In **passive deception**, the researcher omits some critical information about the study. This is quite common as researchers never gives participants all the details of a study, partly because participants probably do not care to know all the details and partly because telling everything about a study would take too much time.

With **active deception**, participants are told that a study is about one thing, but it is really about something else. Stanley Milgram used active deception in his obedience studies.

Researchers often believe that, if people learn what the investigator is studying, they may tailor their behavior, either by being "good" participants who give a researcher what the participant believes the researcher wants or by showing reactance and acting in a way opposite to how they would normally behave. The question of deception is often more relevant in studies of social processes than in studies in domains like perception or learning.

The use of deception in research has spurred significant controversy. Some psychologists believe that deception is unethical and that psychologists should abandon it. Other psychologists believe that some important psychological questions cannot be addressed without deception and that participants recognize that there is a social contract between participants and researchers that allows for some deception within the confines of an experiment. The APA ethics code states that research involving deception can be ethical but discourages its use unless there are no suitable alternatives.

One of the ethical issues associated with deception is that participants cannot provide informed consent if they do not know what a study involves. So a researcher needs to determine the relative risk to participants and whether not knowing about some aspect of the study might constitute a problem. If deception has occurred, it is incumbent upon researchers to **debrief** participants as soon as possible, preferably at the end of the experimental session. The debriefing can consist of **dehoaxing**, which explains the deception, and **desensitization**, which involves remedying any problems that a participant might experience because of the study.

Psychologists who have studied participants' reactions to being deceived have found that, in general, participants do not seem to be bothered by the deception. In fact, many think that psychologists are justified in using deception. Researchers have found that participants are not overly concerned by being given a false **cover story** that inaccurately depicts what a study is going to involve. As a rule, participants are more sensitive to (and less accepting of) being deceived about the role of other persons in the study.

In creating research that involves deception, the investigator needs to determine if the deception violates a person's right to be informed about the study and to participate in it voluntarily. In addition, the psychologist must decide if participants will be embarrassed or otherwise harmed psychologically when they discover that they were deceived.

ETHICAL PRINCIPLES OF THE AMERICAN PSYCHOLOGICAL ASSOCIATION

The American Psychological Association promotes ethical behavior on the part of psychologists acting in various professional roles, including research, the provision of mental health services, and teaching. The APA created its first ethical code in 1953 and has updated it periodically in response to changes in society and the needs of the profession. The current APA ethics code was revised in 2002 and its provisions were updated in 2010.

When an APA member violates the ethics code, the organization may revoke that person's membership. Such instances are rare and when they do occur, they are most frequently associated with clinical and counseling psychology. The APA has well over 100,000 members, so it would not be surprising that, among a group that large, there would be a few individuals who have acted unethically. Fortunately, the vast majority of psychologists are like the population in general: They act with integrity. As noted above, Stanley Milgram's application for APA membership was delayed while the organization scrutinized his research on ethical grounds. When the APA concluded that he had not been unethical in his actions, Milgram was admitted.

The APA has developed a set of General Principles that is intended to guide the professional behavior of psychologists. The five principles are similar to those in the federal government's Belmont Report. They include

(a) beneficence and nonmaleficence, promoting welfare and avoiding harm;
(b fidelity and responsibility, acting professionally to establish the trust of the public and to promote the discipline;
(c) fidelity, promoting the honest and scientific use of psychological knowledge;
(d) justice, ensuring fairness by recognizing one's biases and the limitations of one's competence; and
(e) respect for people's dignity, recognizing the self-determination, privacy, and confidentiality of others.

The General Principles are considered aspirational, meaning that they guide a psychologist's actions. They stand in contrast to the General Standards that involve enforceable rules. If a psychologist does not follow the standards, the APA can sanction that psychologist.

There are ten sections in the ethics standards. They cover a wide range of issues, many of which do not relate specifically to research but that touch on the behavior of researchers. The ten sections of the APA ethics code are listed below:

(a) how to resolve ethical issues
(b) boundaries of competence in professional work
(c) human relations
(d) privacy and confidentiality
(e) advertising and other public statements
(f) record keeping and fees
(g) education and training
(h) research and publication
(i) assessment, and
(j) therapy.

ETHICAL ISSUES UNRELATED TO RESEARCH PARTICIPANTS
Sometimes researchers show lapses in ethics that do not have anything to do with treatment of research participants. There is often a lot of pressure placed on scientists to produce innovative, cutting-edge research, so in some cases, they succumb to that pressure and act unethically.

The U.S. government has an Office of Research Integrity that investigates allegations of ethical violations. Figure 5.2 shows the most common types of violations reported. The single biggest problem is with falsifying data, followed by making up data.

When research does not result in findings that researchers anticipated, some may alter the data to conform to expectations. Much of this research involves biomedical studies that the government has funded. Because it may deal with serious issues associated with causes and treatments of disease, falsifying or making up data may have significant negative consequences. The false findings may keep other researchers from identifying potential causes of a disease, so knowledge about preventing the disease may be delayed; the erroneous information may also keep researchers from studying different treatments that might be effective.

Another ethical issue that is important but that does not have the dire consequences of falsified research results involves plagiarism. Scientists deserve credit for the work they create; they may spend months or years on a single topic of research. It is unethical for another researcher to claim credit for someone else's work or ideas.

Plagiarism can involve using somebody else's words as your own. Sometimes a researcher will knowingly or unknowingly take others' words,

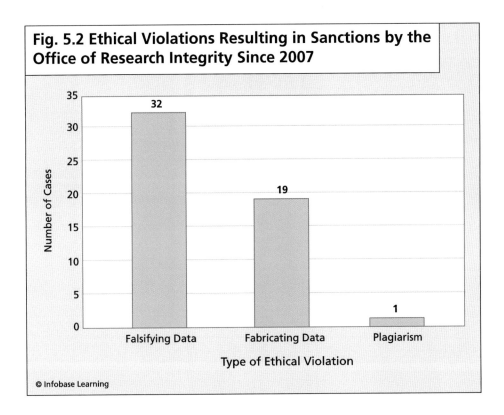

Fig. 5.2 Ethical Violations Resulting in Sanctions by the Office of Research Integrity Since 2007

© Infobase Learning

presenting them as his or her own words. The scientific community regards this as a serious breach of conduct. In other cases, a researcher may steal someone else's ideas and take credit for those ideas. Again, the scientific community considers such behavior as entirely inappropriate. Researchers who engage in such practices may suffer serious consequences; in some cases, plagiarism (whether of words or of ideas) can end a career.

CONCLUSION

Researchers take ethical issues very seriously and follow ethical guidelines in planning and conducting their studies. There are numerous laws that are specifically designed to safeguard the physical and emotional welfare of people who participate in research studies. Beyond such laws regarding the conduct of research, are professional organizations like the American Psychological Association which have developed ethical standards that members must follow.

The laws and professional principles are deemed necessary because there have been several well-known instances in which researchers actively ignored the welfare of participants, with this disregard leading in some cases to injury or death. Most documented examples of violations of ethics have occurred in the realm of biomedical research. There have been a few famous behavioral studies that raised significant ethical issues, but they are the exception rather than the rule.

Further Reading

Rosnow, Ralph L. and Robert Rosenthal. *People Studying People: Artifacts and Ethics in Behavioral Research*. New York, NY US: W. H. Freeman, 1997.

Sales, Bruce D. and Susan Folkman. *Ethics in Research with Human Participants*. Washington, D.C.: American Psychological Association, 2000.

CHAPTER 6

PSYCHOLOGICAL TESTING

ORIGINS OF PSYCHOLOGICAL TESTING

Psychological testing is a significant component of modern psychology. It involves sophisticated and complex approaches to measurement of constructs like intelligence, personality traits, aptitudes, attitudes, and interests. Some of the tests fall within the realm of applied psychology; these include intelligence, psychodiagnostics, or aptitude tests. Others may be more theoretical and are used for basic research. What all of these have in common is an empirical and scientific approach to their development and use.

Originally, psychological testing was purely theoretical, and the tests themselves were very different from psychological tests currently used. The first scientists to test mental processes wanted to understand how people responded when the senses were stimulated. One example of this kind of testing was a study on responses to light intensity: If the intensity of a light is at a certain level and that intensity if doubled, will the light appear twice as bright? Scientists knew that doubling the intensity of a light or a sound did not lead to a doubling of brightness or loudness; the question here was to measure subject response, so they tried to develop predictable relationships between the magnitude of the physical stimulus (e.g., the intensity of the light) and the magnitude of the psychological response (e.g., the brightness of the light).

At about the same time this research was emerging, Charles Darwin's theory of evolution was arousing the scientific world. Darwin's influence on the field of psychology was profound, primarily because his findings were a convincing argument for understanding that mental abilities were subject to the same evolutionary forces as physical traits. According to this view, mental processes were fundamentally biological in nature, could be inherited, and were amenable to study through investigation of the senses. It is for this reasons that the first psychological tests involved **psychophysics**, which is the study of the relationship between a physical stimulus and psychological response.

The German psychologist Wilhelm Wundt (1832–1920) began the systematic study of how people respond to sensory input. Historians generally credit Wundt as the founder of psychology as a discrete discipline, because he established the first laboratory (in 1879) specifically devoted to psychological research. It was here that Wundt conducted "tests" that were meant to establish a systematic connection between events in the external world and how people respond to them.

Around the same time that Wundt established his experimental psychology laboratory, an Englishman named Francis Galton began a systematic study of human sensory capabilities. He collected data on thousands of British citizens, measuring their bodies as well as their visual and auditory abilities.

Expanding on the work of Wundt and Galton, the American psychologist James McKeen Cattell developed a research program that attempted to measure intelligence systematically. In setting up his research, he coined the term "mental test" to refer to his collection of measuring tools and techniques. .

In these early years of psychology, there was no universally agreed upon method of measuring intelligence. Different researchers adopted different approaches, many of which turned out to be unsuccessful. Cattell, for example, devised 50 different measurements that he thought would assess intelligence. In general, these measurements were psychophysical in nature, an approach prompted by the dominant theories of the time, which held that intelligence was biological and evolutionary in nature and thus required biology-oriented tests that could measure sensory processes.

As it turned out, Cattell's measurements did not correlate with one another, meaning that one supposed measure of intelligence did not correspond with a different measure—the two measurements were actually measuring different things. And after considerable research, other psychologists recognized that psychophysical tests were not particularly useful in measuring intelligence. As the dominant theory changed, so did the means of testing.

The first systematic psychological tests in widespread use were intelligence tests created for troops inducted into the U.S. Army in World War I. There were two main forms, one for people who could read and write and the other for people who could not. Although there were significant problems with the tests and the way they were administered, this use of the tests paved the way for the development and use of other psychological tests. The illustration below shows one component of the test designed for people who could not read or write.

The idea of a test for this population was a good one, but the test was problematic. For example, someone illiterate would probably not have known that a

Part of the Army Beta test for illiterate people. The task was to indicate what was missing from each picture. This image is copyrighted by the National Academy of Sciences. It may be from Yerkes, R. M. (1921). *Psychological examining in the United States Army. Memories of the National Academy of Sciences*, Volume 15.

stamp was needed to mail a letter (Item 8). Furthermore, many such individuals lived in rural areas where there was no electricity, so they would not have known that the light bulb was missing a filament (Item 7).

Stephen Jay Gould documented many of the problems associated with both administration and interpretation of these tests. In the end, it is not apparent that the tests had a significant impact on the war effort. Furthermore, the results were subsequently used for political rather than scientific purposes. Nonetheless, in spite of all the problems, the program did establish the viability of administering such a test to a large group of people at the same time.

This chapter features examples of intelligence testing and personality assessment prominently because they represent the most extensive applications of psychological testing. There are many other types of tests, such as employment testing, but these are beyond the scope of this chapter. As previously noted, testing for intelligence was the first systematic program of assessment that psychologists initiated; it began in the 1890s. Since then, psychologists have developed tests for personality, personnel assessment, and attitudes and interests.

INTELLIGENCE TESTS

When the first psychophysical intelligence tests failed to meet anticipated goals, psychologists began searching for better alternatives. Based on the work of Alfred Binet and Théodore Simon in France in 1905, the new generation of tests were verbally oriented and included knowledge-based and problem-solving questions. This approach is not surprising given that Binet and Simon were interested in educational issues, so their theoretical approach involved dimensions important to learning. Modern intelligence tests for adults and older children still consist of components strongly associated with educational tasks.

One of the problems associated with testing intelligence is that we still do not have an adequate definition of intelligence. The basic idea that most psychologists accept is that intelligence involves the ability to learn and to adapt to the environment. Unfortunately, there is still disagreement about the exact nature of the learning and adaptation, so developing a valid test is difficult. In addition, there are cultural considerations within the broad concept of intelligence. In different cultures, important components of intelligence include humility, doing what is right, and maintaining harmonious relationships. These elements are missing entirely from Western intelligence tests.

The basic presupposition behind most approaches to testing intelligence is that more intelligent people know more than less intelligent people and that more intelligent people are better at problem-solving tasks than less intelligent people. From this perspective, it is easy to see why intelligence tests have taken the shape they have. Research on the tests themselves indicates that the scores on many different tests are highly correlated, indicating that they tap similar cognitive abilities.

Individually Administered Intelligence Tests

The first tests of mental functioning were individually administered, with one examiner and one test taker. In Cattell's testing endeavors in the 1890s, measurement took place in his laboratory. Binet and Simon's educational testing also featured a one-on-one methodology as did the American variant of Binet and Simon's test, the Stanford-Binet.

Initial Attempts at Measuring Intelligence

There is still controversy over what constitutes intelligence, with various models positing that there are anywhere from one to 120 major components to intelligence. As a result, there is still disagreement about how best to measure intelligence. Back in the early years of psychology, there was even more uncertainty because nobody had yet attempted to measure it systematically.

James McKeen Cattell included among his measurements dynamometer pressure, the maximum force a person could exert with a squeeze of the hand. The second mode involved measuring how long it took for people to move their right arm 50 centimeters (a little less than two feet). Another measurement was how many consonants a person could remember when Cattell presented them at the rate of two per second. Although we would consider these unusual methods of measuring intelligence, Cattell believed that it was not possible to separate bodily energy and mental energy.

Other attempts to measure intelligence involved assessing the size of a person's head. The reasoning was that if a person had a big head, he or she probably had a big brain. And a big brain would likely mean more intelligence. It did not take long for psychologists to recognize the limitations to this approach, although there are a few psychologists today who still believe that there is a relationship between brain size and intelligence. (Most psychologists disagree.)

Some distinctly odd ideas (from our current perspective) included a measure of intelligence based how long people could stand on their tiptoes and how good their penmanship was. Both of these approaches reflected social beliefs of the day and would not be accepted by psychologists today.

Ironically, the most famous intelligence test, the Stanford-Binet, was derived from the work of two French psychologists who did not claim to be measuring intelligence at all. Their primary motive was to develop a test that would spot children who were likely to fail in school so that these children could be given assistance. American psychologist Lewis Terman translated the test into English and it is now known as the Stanford-Binet test. Ultimately, the Stanford-Binet was adopted in the United States as a test of general intelligence, which Théodore Simon, a co-creator of the original test, believed was counter to the test's original intent.

The intelligence tests pioneered by psychologists David Wechsler beginning in the 1930s have dominated psychology in recent decades. Generally speaking, the tests are oriented either to children or to adults and have gone through a number of revisions. They are individually administered (a psychologist administers the test to one person at any given time).

The most recent intelligence test is the **Wechsler Adult Intelligence Scale-III (WAIS-III).** The Wechsler Scales include a verbal scale and a performance scale. In turn, each of these is divided into subscales. Descriptions of intelligence tests typically give examples to illustrate the type of questions involved. For reasons of test security, the actual questions are not made public, and the examples cited here are taken from public domain content.

Individuals taking the **WAIS-III** test are assessed on what they know; one type of question might ask the test taker to identify the chemical composition of water. Another may ask the test taker to repeat a series of numbers presented orally, at a rate of one per second. In some trials, the task is to repeat these numbers in the same order; in others, test takers may be asked to reverse the order. (Interestingly, this particular test was part of James McKeen Cattell's original measures of intelligence in the failed psychophysical approach to mental testing.)

Other verbal scales involve vocabulary, comprehension, identifying similarities, and verbal arithmetic problems. Some of the performance scales include tasks like identifying what is missing from a picture, arranging pictures in a logical sequence to tell a story, and assembling objects.

Even though psychologists have postulated many components or types of intelligence (e.g., spatial, musical, kinesthetic, logical-mathematical, interpersonal; analytic, creative, practical), they recognize the utility of Wechsler's approach to measuring intelligence with tasks associated with education. The correlations between the verbal scales and high school and college scores tend to be reliable. So if more intelligent people are able to perform better educationally, these correlations provide support for the validity of the intelligence tests.

Another individually administered intelligence test is a descendent of the original test devised by Binet and Simon. The original test was a simple 30-item test. The current version, the Americanized **Stanford-Binet Intelligence Scales: Fifth Edition (SB5),** measures five factors of intelligence recognized in current cognitive psychology: fluid reasoning, knowledge, quantitative reasoning, visual-spatial processing, and working memory. Each of these factors is assessed with verbal and nonverbal tasks, leading to ten subtests on the SB5.

One of the advantages of the SB5 is that its nonverbal component is suitable for people with limited communication skills or knowledge of English. In addition, as psychologist Robert Gregory noted, those who revised this test explicitly recognized some cultural factors that could affect the test score and tried to remedy such limitations. As such, the test now takes into account various religious traditions in addition to the standard personal variables of gender, race, ethnicity, and disability.

Among the problems of the WAIS-III and the SB5 are that they require a highly trained examiner to administer and interpret the test and that the tests themselves are lengthy, in some cases requiring up to two hours. Both factors contribute to the relatively high costs associated with these tests.

One solution to these problems is the **Kaufman Brief Intelligence Test (K-BIT)**. This instrument is shorter than either the WAIS-III or the SB5. It takes 15 to 30 minutes to administer. Scores on the K-BIT correlate highly with those on the other tests, indicating reasonable levels of validity. However, scores on the K-BIT may not be comparable in all cases to those on the highly valid WAIS-III, so psychologists recommend using the K-BIT as an initial screening device to see if further testing is warranted, particularly for people with neurological problems, head injuries, psychiatric problems, and so forth.

Group Intelligence Tests

An alternative to individually administered intelligence tests is the group test that allows simultaneous testing of several or even many people. Such tests arrived on the scene during the first world war, when the U.S. military wanted to assess huge numbers of new recruits. As noted above, there were significant problems with implementation of such testing, but it did demonstrate that group testing was viable and thus led to the development of other group-oriented tests.

It is important to remember that the theory and techniques of testing (and especially group testing) were in their infancy during WWI. Although psychologists were applying the latest ideas and knowledge to testing, they were still ignorant of many aspects of sound mental measurement. In comparison, today's group tests are much more reliable and valid.

Group tests share some features of individual tests. Both types typically assess different components of intelligence and often include a verbal component and a performance component. In fact, the **Multidimensional Aptitude Battery (MAB)** is a group test that was designed to mimic one of Wechsler's tests, the WAIS-R test; additionally, the MAB consists of 10 subtests that mirror most of the WAIS-R subtests.

But there are some notable differences between individual and group tests. One involves format. Individual tests generally contain open-ended questions that allowed the examinee to respond however he or she thinks appropriate, whereas group tests generally involve closed-ended questions, specifically multiple-choice items. Somewhat related to the matter of formatting is the matter of scoring: Individual tests are scored by the examiner, whereas the group tests are typically machine scored. Thus, one of the advantages of the group tests include less expense and time involved in administration and scoring.

The disadvantages include possible problems with interpretation of individual test scores. With large-scale testing, it is possible for people (often students) with low motivation or poor reading skills to perform poorly on a test even when their intelligence levels are at normal or above-normal levels. With large groups, those administering the tests may not attend to the potential reasons for such low scores, so such individuals may be classified inappropriately. Because of these limitations, psychologists recommend evaluating low scores and referring people with low scores for further testing.

Social and Cultural Issues in Intelligence Testing

Psychologists generally conceive of intelligence as the ability to learn, to problem solve, and to adapt to the environment. In the abstract, this set of abilities captures how most people understand intelligence. If you look at intelligence tests, however, it is the ability to learn that predominates. Problem solving and adapting are not well represented because they are very difficult to assess in a testing situation. Furthermore, the historical traditions in intelligence testing have often focused on educational skills, and each new test that emerges is generally validated through comparison to previous tests.

Which approach is the best or the most valid? The answer to that question is that there is no single correct answer. That is, psychologists can measure intelligence in many different ways, depending on the purpose of the measurement. One of the most common uses is to diagnose a person who may have intellectual deficits. That is the purpose of the tests that David Wechsler envisioned when he created the various versions of the Wechsler Scales. Psychologists agree that such verbal and performance tests can be quite useful in spotting people with problems.

Unfortunately, the spectrum of intellectual abilities far exceeds the limited scope that characterizes standardized intelligence tests. Psychologist Howard Gardner has identified multiple domains that he believes represent different components of intelligence. For example, he has argued that musical intelligence, interpersonal (i.e., social) intelligence, and intrapersonal intelligence (i.e., knowledge of oneself) and others are legitimate domains of intelligence. He continues to identify additional domains of intelligence.

Gardner's multiple intelligences sound like an attractive way to describe the constellation of intellectual skills, but there is not much empirical support for his theory. His various domains of intelligence tend to intercorrelate, which psychologists have interpreted to mean that there is a basic, general component to intelligence rather than the multiple dimensions Gardner suggests. Neuroscientists have also studied his theory to see if there might be support for it with respect to the functioning of the brain; to date, there is little such support.

Moreover, Gardner has not really defined intelligence in a way that would allow systematic testing of his theory.

Another theory of intelligence is Robert Sternberg's triarchic (three-faceted) theory, which stipulates that it is useful to conceptualize intelligence as practical, creative, and analytical. That is, some people may be highly intelligent in practical areas but are not particularly creative or educationally smart (i.e., analytical). As with Gardner's theory, Sternberg's triarchic theory extends beyond customary views of intelligence and has shown promise in research by him and his colleagues, but the overall theory still awaits extensive validation through research.

Because intelligence has such important social connotations, however, people pay a lot of attention to it. This is undoubtedly why theories like Gardner's and Sternberg's may initially gain more acceptance among the nonscientific public than among psychologists. Both ideas have an intuitive appeal that seems to make very good sense. In addition, everybody knows someone with supposedly normal intelligence who is startlingly proficient in a particular domain. It seems reasonable to conclude that the domain could represent a type of intelligence. However, until researchers can investigate this potential intelligence, it would be premature to conclude that the domain represents a single, independent kind of intelligence.

A topic related to different types of intelligence is that of individual learning styles. Claims have been made that some people are visual learners, others verbal learners, and still others auditory learners; in addition, some educators believe that certain people learn better by analysis and others by listening. This breakdown of learning styles relates to different types of intelligence in the sense of effective information processing. Even though educators have widely adopted these views, there is still little empirical evidence that students learn better in one mode than in another, although they may show preferences for one mode, may display different skills associated with various learning styles, and may believe that it is their most effective way of learning.

Because of the popularity of the concept of intelligence, you can find tests claiming to measure intelligence on various Internet sites. These tests have typically not been standardized or studied for their psychometric properties. Consequently, it is undoubtedly not wise to consider them as being legitimate psychological tests. Their value is for entertainment rather than for serious psychological purposes.

The Search for Culture-Fair Intelligence Tests

In some cultures, people use the concept of intelligence synonymously with educationally oriented abilities, like verbal and mathematical skills. This approach is common in the United States. In other cultures, intelligence has a social component related to a person's ability to work effectively in groups.

With such differences in the way people think about intelligence, it is no surprise that a given approach to measurement of intelligence in one culture may not be useful in another culture or country. Psychologists know that there are significant problems with measurement of intelligence within a single country, especially when they attempt to examine people from different subcultures within that country. The problem is magnified across countries and across languages.

Sociologist Adrian Dove created a pretend intelligence test to illustrate how people from a given, "disadvantaged" culture might generate low scores on a test. His test had 30 knowledge-based items. One example that illustrates the culture-knowledge bias follows:

Which word is most out of place here?

(a) splib
(b) blood
(c) gray
(d) spook
(e) black

The answer is (c) gray. When Dove first created the test over four decades ago, people in his "disadvantaged" culture could not give the correct answer. In this case, the "disadvantaged" culture was white. The answer choices would easily have been recognized by many people within America's black cultural community of the time. Undoubtedly, fewer people would be able to choose the correct answer today because language and word meanings change. Dove used questions like this to show that what might be an obvious fact to people of normal intelligence from one group may be (and often is) entirely incomprehensible to people from another group.

This example underscores the fact that intelligence tests are largely based on different kinds of knowledge. If a certain person or group of people are (or are not) exposed to the knowledge being tested, test scores will be biased either in favor of or against them. To counter this problem, numerous psychologists have tried to develop **culture-free tests**. Such tests would, in theory, be free of systematic bias based on knowledge or culture. Unfortunately, nobody has yet succeeded in creating such a test.

A logical alternative to a culture-free test would be a **culture-fair test**. Such an instrument would measure people from any culture without introducing bias associated with cultural differences. Unfortunately, such a test also seems impossible to design. One reason for this is that people from different cultures place different values on various skills and abilities. Furthermore, all tests are based, to some degree, on what a person has learned and how it was learned. The leads to related problem: Somebody has to create test items, but any individual test designer's choice of what constitutes "reasonable" questions will more than likely introduce bias. So the content of a test is always going to favor some groups and hinder others. The implication is that tests of intelligence are always going to be culturally bound. With that as a given, psychologists and educators need to make sure that tests are as appropriate as possible for the people who take them.

Psychologists with expertise in **psychometrics** (that is, the statistical characteristics of tests) have identified two issues that are important for understanding cultural effects of tests. The first issue is **test bias**. This is a statistical concept that is amenable to empirical testing. That is, researchers can find out through research if a test is biased and, if it is biased, whom it favors and whom it impedes. The second issue, one that is more social and philosophical than statistical in nature, is whether tests are culturally fair. Fairness is not a scientific concept but a concept based on social judgments about which uses of intelligence tests are in the best interest of society.

PERSONALITY TESTS
Psychologists are often interested in finding out about an individual's personality traits, motivation, personal adjustment, and psychopathology. To this end, they have created a large number of tests based on a wide variety of theories and methodologies. It would be impossible to review every major test in this brief presentation, so this discussion will concentrate on the major classes of tests, with examples showing how psychologists use them.

Projective Tests
In general, **projective tests** involve items like ambiguous pictures, inkblots, or incomplete sentences to which an examinee responds. The tests are open-ended in the sense that the person taking the test provides his or her interpretation of the given item. Subsequently, the psychologist interprets the person's responses in order to make a judgment about the individual's personality characteristics, motivations, and so forth.

Probably the best-known projective test is the **Rorschach Test**. It consists of 10 cards featuring inkblots that an examinee describes and interprets. This test is based on the psychodynamic theory of Sigmund Freud, which is true of a number of other projective tests as well.

One of the criticisms of the Rorschach test is that its function is not entirely clear. Psychologists have used it for obtaining psychiatric diagnoses, but it has also been used for other purposes, including personality assessments. Research on its psychometric properties (i.e., how well it functions in relation to its intended purpose) generates low scores on reliability and validity. (Psychologists use the term **reliability** when explaining whether a test generates

The Rorschach Inkblot Test

According to Freudian theory, a psychologist can fathom hidden dimensions of an individual's personality through interpretation of statements that individual makes. This theory specifically notes that when a person encounters an ambiguous stimulus and attempts to tell what it means to him or her, the interpretation can reveal fundamental aspects of the personality. A very good example of such an "ambiguous stimulus" is an image from Rorschach Inkblot Test.

The most frequent interpretation involves animals, often people or four-legged animals. The red parts of the inkblot are often interpreted as blood and can pertain to feelings of anger or anxiety about physical harm. Psychologists interpret not only the content of a person's responses but also how the person incorporates color and texture of the images into those responses.

Normally, test makers are quite protective of the items on their tests, primarily because they do not want people to take the test with advance knowledge of the materials on the test. Some psychologists were understandably annoyed and upset when the online encyclopedia Wikipedia published the inkblots. There were no copyright issues involved because the test was published over 70 years ago, and the copyright has expired, but these psychologists felt that Wikipedia's decision to make the images universally accessible may have diminished their usefulness as testing instruments

consistent measurements and **validity** when explaining whether something tests usefully that which it is supposed to test.)

Researchers continue to refine the Rorschach test in order to improve it, but it is still seen by psychometricians as less valid than more objective personality tests. To overcome the limitations of the Rorschach, psychologists have developed several new tests. One example is a new set of inkblots created by psychologist Wayne Holtzman. This set has 45 inkblots (compared to the 10 on the Rorschach) and boasts a simplified administration and scoring system. Initial research suggests that it may be a very effective tool in diagnosing schizophrenia, but it may take several years to determine its reliability and validity. An entirely different projective approach involves completion techniques. An examinee's task here is to fill in the details about an incomplete stimulus by telling what came before the stimulus, what is happening at the time the stimulus is in play, and what the outcome will be. A common stimulus in such tests is a sentence fragment (something like *My most important goal in life is _____*). During the session, the subject may respond to up to 100 such sentences, depending on the particular test.

There are numerous sentence completion tests, many of them not standardized or normed to a specific population. So it is difficult to assess the reliability and validity of such instruments. The research that has appeared has revealed modest levels of reliability, leading some psychologists to recommend that these instruments be used for research but not for psychodiagnosis.

Another widely known projective test is the **Thematic Apperception Test (TAT)**, which was developed in the 1930s by psychologists Henry Murray and Christiana Morgan to test imagination, to identify the strength or weakness of a subject's needs (e.g., need for achievement), and to determine the degree to which the subject feels beset by external forces. The stimuli in this test include 30 pictures; the examinee responds to 20 of these and tells a story about these 20. Based on the story, a psychologist will attempt to understand a person's drives and motivations. Today, there is no standard way of administering the TAT and no consistent approach to scoring and interpreting the responses. As such, it is difficult to assess the test's reliability and validity.

Assessment of Projective Tests

Research has shown that projective tests have notable and important limitations. In some cases, the reliability level is acceptable, which means that an interpretation of one person's responses will lead to similar interpretations with repeated testing. But the validity component of projective tests is more tenuous. Although some research shows a small degree of validity exists in a few of these tests, the overall picture shows little (and sometimes less) to suggest that the majority of them test what they claim to test.

Projective tests are also relatively costly, both in terms of time and money. Only highly qualified psychologists can administer them. In fact, some tests require specific training for adequate administration. Thus, there are practical issues of administration, scoring, and interpretation that relate to their use.

Nonetheless, clinicians continue to defend and use projective tests in spite of their documented limitations. And even though there are other, more effective tests projective tests are used often—five of the fifteen most commonly used psychological tests in the United States are projective tests; within the top seven of that group of fifteen, four are projective.

Theory-Based Self-Report Inventories

Projective tests are typically psychodynamic in orientation, based at some level on Freudian ideas. Such instruments are open ended, allowing examinees to take a response in any direction they want. Interpretation requires extensive training and expertise on the part of the person administering the test.

Alternatives to these tests are theory-based tests that make use of forced-choice formats, which require respondents to choose from among a set of fixed options. For example, Murray and Morgan's theory of needs led to the development of the Edwards Personal Preference Schedule (EPPS), which consists of 210 pairs of statements and requires a respondent to select one statement from each pair. Both statements in such pairs are set up to be equally desirable (or equally undesirable). The content of each statement is based on one of the needs in Murray and Morgan's theory, and respondents make their selections based on statement content they identify with most closely. Examples of the kinds of paired statements that may appear on the EPPS are (a) *I like working outdoors* and (b) *I enjoy creative tasks.*

Another theoretically oriented test, perhaps the most widely used test with nonpsychiatric groups, is the **Myers-Briggs Type Indicator (MBTI)**. The MBTI is based on Carl Jung's theory of personality types. Interestingly, the test has found widespread acceptance in business applications even though most research psychologists do not regard Jungian theory as being particularly useful in understanding the personality. Scores on the test reflect four independent dimensions: Extraversion-Introversion, Sensing-Intuition, Thinking-Feeling, and Judging-Perceptive.

Results of the MBTI characterize people as being at one end of the continuum for each dimension, so they would be reported as either extraverted or introverted, even though the raw scores occur on a continuum. With four dimensions and two options on each dimension, the structure of the personality is reported as one of 16 different types.

Quantitatively oriented psychologists have been quite critical of the MBTI. Research on its effectiveness has revealed adequate reliability, but investigators have conducted relatively few studies of its validity.

Other theoretically based self-report inventories exist. They have various strengths and weaknesses and varying degrees of reliability and validity.

Criterion-Keyed Inventories

A second category of objectively scored tests is theoretically neutral. These are the **criterion-keyed inventories,** which include items that effectively discriminate among different personality or psychopathological types. These instruments involve statements that are not tied to any theory and thus do not relate to Freudian, Jungian, or other theoretical ideas.

The most widely used of these inventories is the **Minnesota Multiphasic Personality Inventory (MMPI).** Currently in its second version, this test consists of 567 True-False items that ask about the person responding. The MMPI has ten scales (see Table 6.1) that assess clinical diagnoses of such pathologies as depression, hysteria, paranoia, schizophrenia, and others.

The test items do not need to refer to symptoms of depression, paranoia, or any other psychiatric problem in any obvious way. Instead, the items are chosen for the test based on how depressed, paranoid, and other people respond to them, regardless of the actual content. So items like *I would like to be a writer* or *I enjoy reading about science* appear even though neither one seems to be

TABLE 6.1
MMPI-2 Scales and What They Measure

Scale	What it Measures
Hypochondriasis	Preoccupation with physical problems and conditions
Depression	Sadness, hopelessness
Hysteria	Repression, immaturity, awareness of vulnerability
Psychopathic deviate	Feelings about authority, impulsiveness, anger, conflict
Masculinity-Femininity	Stereotypical gender interests
Paranoia	Hostility, mistrust, feelings of suspicion
Psychasthenia	Anxiety, obsession, worry, doubts
Schizophrenia	Altered thought processes, alienation from society
Hypomania	Energy level, agitation, excitability
Social introversion	Shyness, orientation to others

associated with a particular diagnosis. This approach is strictly correlational. That is, there is no obvious reason for an item to be associated with a diagnosis; it just is.

An additional feature of the MMPI that does not exist in most other inventories is a set of scales that do not pertain to clinical diagnoses. The results of the MMPI indicate the number of omitted items and items with two responses; the output also presents scales that indicate whether the person taking the test is trying to look good or is faking answers in an attempt to appear either more or less well adjusted. The advantage of such scales is that the psychologist can evaluate how useful the test is in the diagnostic process.

The MMPI has shown significant strengths in helping psychologists diagnose people with potential psychiatric problems and has been shown to be useful in practical areas such as identifying people with a history of sexual abuse, prediction of surgical outcomes, and treatment of criminals. Its reliability and validity levels are quite high, one of the reasons that it is the dominant instrument for assessing and diagnosing psychological problems.

There are many other criterion-keyed inventories, but one that is particularly worth mentioning is the **California Psychological Inventory (CPI)**. Unlike the majority of other tests, this inventory assesses dimensions of the normal personality. There are 20 personality scales on the CPI, including such dimensions as dominance, sociability, empathy, tolerance, and intellectual efficiency.

Like the MMPI, the CPI contains True-False items. There are 462 statements, with almost 200 coming directly from the MMPI. The CPI also includes scales to detect whether people are responding randomly or trying to appear either more or less normal. The reliability and validity estimates are generally high for the CPI, although some scales can show low validity levels.

Befitting its origin as a test for normal populations, the CPI has proven to be useful in applications dealing with everyday functioning. Research has shown that the CPI is successful in predicting performance in high school, college, and medical school. It is also effective in other practical areas like predicting leadership ability.

TEST DEVELOPMENT AND VALIDATION

By the time a test taker sees a test, everything on that test seems logical and straightforward. In reality, however, the practice of test creation is enormously complex and technical; in fact, it takes considerable time, effort, and revision to develop a test idea into a useful instrument. Consider, for example, that it took almost a decade to produce the final form of the second version of the MMPI.

Developing Questions

When a team of psychologists begins the process of test construction, they must address several critical questions. For instance, how varied should test items be? If the test is going to assess knowledge, then there should be a fairly heterogeneous representation of relevant topics. On the other hand, if the test is supposed to assess a single attitude, the questions would be much narrower in focus.

Another issue is length of the test. The final version of the test should be long enough to provide adequate measurement of the construct being assessed without being so long that a person taking the test becomes bored or tired before completing it. It is common in test construction for psychologists to create many more questions than they anticipate using. The reason for this excess is that it is not clear at the onset which items will be most useful and function most effectively in measuring what the psychologists intend to assess. This uncertainty in test development is typical. The original MMPI, for example, had over 1,000 personality statements before it reached its final form. When refined and whittled down, the final set of items constituted a highly reliable and valid test. Still another issue in test development involves item format. Tests of knowledge frequently use objectively scored, multiple-choice questions because they are easy to score either by a person or via computer, and they can be administered to groups efficiently. The potential disadvantages of such items are the difficulty in constructing good items that will adequately test conceptual knowledge rather than simply factual knowledge. Personality inventories are likely to use questions that a person will answer with either *True* or *False* responses or select an answer that shows where he or she falls on a continuum.

For more subjectively scored tests, such as the projective tests, creating effective test items that generating open-ended responses can also be challenging. The test stimuli must induce responses that pertain to underlying personality constructs that are relevant to and important for a particular theory.

Testing the Test

After the psychologists create the questions, they need to test the test. This process involves generating a sample of people to take the test, then assessing whether the responses produce useful results. So if the test is supposed to assess knowledge, the psychologists must gauge how well people performed on the test in comparison to some other valid measurement of intelligence.

For personality inventories designed to help with psychodiagnosis, psychologists will administer their test to people with known characteristics or conditions (e.g., a group of people who are clinically depressed and a different group that are not depressed) to see if the grouped responses are predictably different from one another. Samples are often very diverse and very large, with thousands of people taking the test.

An important measure of a test is its reliability. With regard to measurements, it is important to understand that reliability means repeatability or consistency. It does not mean useful or effective. Just because a test results in the same score for a person with repeated administrations, it does not mean that the test is assessing what the psychologist wants it to test.

There are different forms of reliability. One is **test-retest reliability**. This form of reliability involves repeated administration of the test to the same individuals. If the test shows test-retest reliability, people will achieve about the same scores each time they take the test. Reliability measurements are correlations; psychologists regard test-retest reliability correlation coefficients as acceptable when the value of the coefficient is at least .80 and preferably over .90, although decisions about acceptable levels require judgment on a case by case basis.

Another measure of reliability involves the internal consistency of a test. That is, do the items in an inventory tend to measure the same thing. One such reliability measurement is **split-half reliability**, which involves correlating two equivalent halves of the same test. The most common approach is to correlate even- and odd-numbered items. An alternative approach to this kind of reliability is the use of **coefficient alpha**, which is obtained by find the average of all possible split-half coefficients for a test.

Psychometricians have continually worked to refine the various approaches to computing reliability. There is no single "best" approach to measuring reliability. Different types of tests that measure different constructs may require different measures of reliability. What is important is to recognize is that reliability involves consistency or repeatability of scores.

Acceptable reliability is necessary for good measurement, but it is not sufficient by itself. What is ultimately more important than reliability is **validity**, which is a measure of the utility of a test for a given purpose. As with reliability, measurements of validity take several forms.

Content validity gauges whether the constellation of questions on a test represents the universe of behaviors or knowledge to which the test relates. For instance, a classroom test on social psychology should consist of a set of questions that covers the spectrum of concepts related to social psychology. Such a test will have content validity to the extent that the small sampling of questions adequately represents all possible questions. On a personality test, questions should present a representative sample of behaviors or ideation associated with some dimension of personality. For knowledge tests and for personality inventories, it is generally impossible to develop a test that would measure every single aspect of the domain. First of all, we do not know all aspects of any domain and, secondly, a test would be unreasonably long even if we could include every possible question about that domain. Judgments of content validity are often made by experts who determine whether the questions are adequate for their purpose. It is difficult to quantify content validity.

A second type of validity is **criterion-related validity**, which relates to the ability to make accurate predictions based on test scores. Predictions can involve **concurrent validity**, predictions of some behavior occurring at roughly the same time as a person takes a test. In contrast, **predictive validity** relates to predictions about future behaviors.

The final type of validity that we will deal with here is **construct validity**, which relates to how well a test measures the concept it is supposed to measure. Thus, one scale of the Holtzman Inkblot Test (HIT) is designed to measure schizophrenia. According to the research on this test, there is agreement between scores on the test and independent measures of schizophrenia. In one particular study, the HIT was highly successful (but not perfect) in identifying people previously diagnosed as schizophrenic and in classifying as normal a set of people who were not diagnosed as schizophrenic.

If a test does not show high levels of reliability, it cannot be valid. If reliability is at a high level, the test may be valid, but its validity needs to be verified. In contrast, a high level of validity guarantees that reliability will be good.

CONCLUSION

The first psychological tests measured mental functioning and, although they were not successful as tests of intelligence, they led to intelligence tests that psychologists recognized as effective. The initial tests were psychophysical in nature, but as a result of the groundbreaking work of Alfred Binet and Théodore Simon in France, they were gradually replaced by tests more oriented toward educational tasks.

American psychologist Lewis Terman modified the work of Binet and Simon and created tests that, in theory, provided an overall measurement of intelligence. Current tests are intellectual descendants of the original tests. Today, however, psychologists speculate that there are different components to intelligence although many of them are correlated with one another. As a result, some contemporary psychologists have suggested that there is a single component underlying intelligence that is related to the newly proposed dimensions.

Another major use of psychological tests is for personality assessment, which is often linked to diagnosing psychological problems. Test formats can involve projective tests that allow examinees to generate their own responses to test items. Other formats provide a set of fixed responses from which an examinee must make a selection. The more objective formats are generally regarded as more psychometrically sound.

In order to create tests, psychologists have to make many decisions about content, format, and length. After constructing an initial test, they evaluate how well it functions for the intended purpose. The major criteria involved in this assessment are reliability (i.e., consistency) and validity (i.e., usefulness).

Further Reading

Gould, Stephen J. *The Mismeasure of Man*. New York, NY, US: W. W. Norton, 1981.

CHAPTER 7

MEASUREMENT IN PSYCHOLOGY

THE IMPORTANCE OF MEASUREMENT

Numbers are an important fact of life. In contemporary society, it seems that people try to measure just about everything. A number of years ago, a major polling organization even attempted to estimate the number of people claiming to have been abducted by aliens.[1]

One of the most ambitious measurements in any given country is the census. In the United States, a census is taken every 10 years. From the first census taken after the nation was founded, the data collected have never been completely accurate. And even with modern technology and methodology, this situation does not seem to be getting any better.

The problem begins with the basic fact the census does not produce an accurate count of the number of people living in this country. And if we cannot count the number of people, which in theory is relatively straightforward, it is easy to see how difficult it is to measure more abstract concepts, like attitudes, degrees of depression, intelligence, knowledge, and so forth.

---

[1] The value that the pollsters came up with, based on a sample of about 6,000 people, was that about two percent of the American population had claimed to be abducted. At the time the poll was taken, this would have constituted about 5 million people—a figure even more implausible than the claim of abduction itself.

Measurement is a critical tool for society (and for individuals within the society), one that can answer questions, solve problems, and provide data that can help society (and individuals) to function more smoothly and efficiently. While it may be difficult to measure things (even tangible things), it is important to do so and critical to do it well. Census results, for instance, are not just about counting people; based on the numbers, the census can help identify population centers where we are going to need hospitals, schools, roads, water supplies, and other very important services. Other practical outcomes of statistical measurements are even broader, including the development of social policies.

The Worst Social Statistic Ever

"Every year since 1950, the number of American children gunned down has doubled."

This statistic has been dubbed "The Worst Social Statistic Ever" by sociologist Joel Best. Although the claim was based on reasonable data, this data fell into the category that Best referred to as *mutant statistics*. But how, one might ask, did they became "mutant"?

The original research data generated on this issue were published by the Children's Defense Fund and reflected a statistical analysis that was reasonably accurate. Later, another researcher inadvertently misstated what the original researchers had said.

The original claim, although it included verbiage that was similar to that in the distorted claim, accurately reported that "The number of American children killed each year by guns has doubled since 1950." If you juxtapose the two statements, it is easy to see that there is a world of difference between them.

Original: "The number of American children killed each year by guns has doubled since 1950."

Distorted: "Every year since 1950, the number of American children gunned down has doubled."

The distorted claim is more than wrong. It absolutely cannot be true. Suppose that during the baseline year of measurement (1950) one child was killed by gunshot. It would follow that in 1951, there would be 2 children killed by gunshot; in 1952, there would be 4; in 1953, there would be 8; and so on. Table

WHERE DO NUMBERS COME FROM?

The problem with measurement in psychology is that it a remarkably difficult task. The measurements may themselves be problematic, sometimes because of inaccurate numbers and sometimes because the numbers do not really measure what people want them to measure. In other cases, numbers may be selectively used by people who want to advance a particular argument or theory. Numbers that don't agree with their hypotheses or run counter to their claims may simply be ignored. And sometimes numbers are poorly interpreted because the person assigned to interpret them does not really understand them.

TABLE 7.1.
Number of Presumed Deaths by Decade According to the "Worst Social Statistic Ever"

Year	Rounded number of deaths	Number of deaths
1950	One	1
1960	One thousand	1,024
1970	One million	1,048,576
1980	One billion	1,073,741,824
1990	One trillion	1,099,511,627,776
2000	One quadrillion	1,125,899,906,842,624
2010	One quintillion	1,152,921,504,606,846,976

7.1 shows how many such gunshot deaths there would be in America based on the statistic.

The numbers are clearly ludicrous. To begin with, it is terribly tragic but very unlikely that there was only a single child killed by gunshot in 1950. And given that there are roughly six billion people on earth today, it is impossible for over one quintillion children to die this way. This is a good illustration of how a reasonable statistic became an unreasonable mutant. Unfortunately, sometimes statistics taking on a mutant form persist as if they were accurate. This can be a problem for many reasons, one of which is that a good overall argument (e.g., for gun control) could lose credibility because of a single misreading or misstatement of statistical fact.

Sociologist Joel Best has pointed out that statistics can inform or can mislead, depending on the care associated with either generating or interpreting the data. Based on this interpretation, measurements can fail for a number of reasons. Best also joked that "a bad statistic is harder to kill than a vampire." The previous sidebar illustrates just how bad statistics can be.

Joel Best also noted that numbers are not neutral bits of information. They exist and have meaning because of the decisions made by researchers in their investigations. In connection with this, there are three important questions to ask any time you see numerical data:

First, who collected the data? People do not collect data for no reason; they often have political agendas or points they want to make. You cannot always count on numbers being valid indicators of what people claim they measure.

Second, what did the researchers count? Several years ago, investigators wanted to find out how many adolescents smoke cigarettes. But what constitutes *adolescence*? Researchers might regard anybody from age 12 to 19 as an adolescent. But a 12-year-old is much different from a 19-year-old. In addition, what does it mean *to smoke*? Is a smoker someone who takes a single puff in one month? Someone who smokes a single cigarette a day? Someone who smokes multiple packs a day? Or all of the above? The researchers in this case counted a single puff on a cigarette within the past 30 days as constituting smoking. But most people would view a person taking a single puff that may never recur as very different from a multiple-pack-per-day smoker.

Third, where did the numbers come from? Data comes about because people choose a certain methodology. Generally, the data come about from a sample that is supposed to represent a larger population. If the sample does not represent the population, the data won't either.

In the end, it is important to remember that researchers have to make decisions on how they define their terms and how they collect their numbers. Each researcher makes his or her own choices. Professional researchers try to remain as objective as they can, but personal preferences, assumptions, and beliefs always influence the final outcome. Because of potential problems with data, researchers who publish their research in professional journals typically provide considerable detail about the numbers they are working with and where those numbers came from.

OPERATIONAL DEFINITIONS
In this chapter, you will see how hard it is to conduct good psychological research because measuring abstract, psychological states is difficult. Psychologists (and

other social and behavioral scientists) have shown considerable creativity and ingenuity in their attempts to measure important psychological and behavioral concepts. So as you read about the difficulties associated with making good measurements, you should realize that there are pitfalls to be avoided, while at the same time, it is indeed possible to study difficult issues successfully in scientific, meaningful ways.

One of the concepts important in psychological measurement is **operational definition**. Sometimes psychologists want to measure very abstract things, such as depression, happiness, or amount of learning that has occurred. On an everyday level, we recognize what these words mean, but scientists need to measure them in objective ways that other scientists can understand and use. This is where operational definitions come in. Operational definitions are statements of how an abstract concept will be measured.

For example, suppose you wanted to determine if one person was happier than another. The first step would be to figure out how to measure happiness. There are different approaches you could take to do this. Among the simplest would be to ask the people how happy they are. In one study on this issue, psychologists Frank Andrews and Stephen Withey asked people, "How do you feel about your life as a whole?" Respondents answered on a 7-point scale with answers that ranged from *delighted* to *terrible*.

More recent inventories of happiness include multiple items. For example, the 29-item Oxford Happiness Inventory (OHI) includes items like "I have lots of fun." Respondents were likely to show high levels of agreement with this item. On the other hand, they were less likely to report agreement with items such as "I have boundless levels of energy."

Psychologists often ask people to respond to questions with pre-selected answers on a scale of 1 to some number (e.g., 7); such instruments are called **Likert-type scales.** The number that a person chooses on a scale like the OHI is an operational definition of happiness. In this approach, psychologists recognize that happiness is a complex internal state that they cannot measure directly. So a person's rating on the Likert-type scale is used as a reasonable alternate measurement.

As a rule, psychologists endeavoring to measure complex abstract concepts try to develop measuring instruments that are as short and as simple as possible. The sidebar below presents a 6-item inventory created by psychologist Stephen Joseph and his colleagues to assess happiness. This inventory could be useful for research conducted with groups. The sidebar also indicates how psychologists go about developing useful measurements. In the end, the researchers concluded that their short test provided an adequate operational definition of happiness.

Psychologists recognize the utility of rating scales to measure abstract concepts. That is why they agree that scores on an inventory like the OHI are sensible representations of happiness. Everybody recognizes that the measurement is not perfect, but if it provides a useful score that researchers can use to answer questions meaningfully, investigators will adopt that measurement. At the same time, they continue to search for better measurements.

With the advent of neurological techniques that allow measurement of brain activity, it might be possible to identify specific brain regions associated with happiness. For example, Hidehiko Takahashi and colleagues have identified cortical regions associated with joy—the ventral striatum and insula/operculum, which are the key sites processing of pleasure stimuli.

It is important to remember, however, that although researchers might be able to identify the brain regions associated with feelings like happiness, it does not mean that the neural response is the same as happiness. Happiness is a psychological response; it may be associated with specific neural activity, but neural activity is biological and the experience of happiness is psychological. The measurement of brain activity is another way to operationally define happiness, a way to get a precise measurement of a biological action associated with psychology.

Psychologists may agree that these types of measurements of happiness are useful, but in some other domains, such measurements are still subject to discussion. For example, suppose a researcher wanted to measure aggression. Typically, aggression is studied experimentally by devising a task that people think they can do but that the experimenter prevents them from doing, usually by having somebody else keep them from completing the assigned task. The people attempting to complete the assigned task feel frustrated and may

The Short Depression–Happiness Scale

Psychologist Stephen Joseph and his colleagues started with a 25-item inventory to measure happiness. They tested 137 participants to see how they responded. Based on statistical analysis, they found that six items in their inventory worked well in identifying levels of happiness (versus depression).

The researchers then examined whether the scale produced reliable responses. They looked at data from three studies and discovered that the six-item inventory produced consistent results when people completed it more than once.

Finally, the psychologists examined participants' responses on their inventory in conjunction with other psychological inventories to see if the responses on the short test showed the same patterns as they did in other valid inventories. The researchers found that the short item would be a useful, quick assessment of happiness.

show aggression, which is generally defined as a response by a person who wants to harm somebody else. So how could a researcher come up with a valid way to measure aggression as it is defined? Ethical considerations prevent investigators from letting one person harm another, so researchers must find another way.

One was for researchers to approach this is to ask the frustrated person to write something about the individual who caused the frustration. If the frustrated person writes derogatory comments, these are taken as a sign of aggression. However, because it is not clear that negative comments about another person are really intended to harm that person, the behavior may not reflect true aggression.

TABLE 7.2
The Short Depression-Happiness Scale (SDHS)

A number of statements that people have made to describe how they feel are given below. Please read each one and tick the box which best describes how frequently you felt that way in the past seven days, including today. Some statements describe positive feelings and some describe negative feelings. You may have experienced both positive and negative feelings at different times during the past seven days.

Item	Never	Rarely	Sometimes	Often
I felt dissatisfied with my life				
I felt happy				
I felt cheerless				
I felt pleased with the way I am				
I felt that life was enjoyable				
I felt that life was meaningless				

Note: Items 1, 3, and 6 are reverse scored. (In normal scoring, if *Never* is given a score of 1, it will be converted to a score of 4 in reverse scoring on this scale. Similarly, *Rarely* in normal scoring is 2, but it would be a 3 in reverse scoring, and so forth.)

Source of copyrighted material: Joseph, Stephen, P. Alex Linley, Jake Harwood, Christopher Alan Lewis, and Patrick McCollam. 2004. Rapid assessment of well-being: The short depression-happiness scale (SDHS). *Psychology and Psychotherapy: Theory, Research and Practice* 77, (4) (Dec):463–478.

Simulated electrical shocks are another technique that researchers have used as a measure of aggression. But psychologist Joel Lieberman and his colleagues have pointed out several drawbacks to this approach. One drawback is that this technique requires equipment that may be quite expensive. In addition, Institutional Review Boards are likely to deny a researcher permission to use electric shocks in conducting research. Furthermore, many people know about Stanley Milgram's obedience research. Because nobody actually received shocks in Milgram's experiments, some people may assume that these are not real shocks and are harmless. Moreover, some people may administer shocks as a sign of their competitiveness, not their aggression.

Because simulated electric shock research is clearly problematic, researchers have had to be creative. One novel and clever approach was used by Joel Lieberman and his colleagues. During the study, the researches asked participants to pour hot (i.e., spicy) sauce into a cup for another person to drink. Depending on the stimulus (i.e., if participants thought they had previously been given foul-tasting food by that other person), they poured more hot sauce into the cup for the person to drink. The study was a little more complicated than described here, but the researchers found that in conditions that were likely to lead to aggressive behavior, participants wanted another person to drink more of the hot sauce. As such, the psychologists concluded that they had created a valid operational definition of a person's level of aggressiveness.

The researchers were confident in their measurement because their research results supported their theoretically based hypotheses and because the correlation between hot sauce allocation and scores on an aggression questionnaire by Buss and Perry was significant. Their approach received additional support from researcher Özlem Ayduk and colleagues who showed that people who were sensitive to social rejection administered more hot sauce than did people who were not particularly sensitive to such rejection.

SCALES OF MEASUREMENT

Over half a century ago psychologist S.S. Stevens wrote an influential paper on statistical measurement. In this paper, Stevens asserted that the type of statistics that researchers can use depended on the mathematical sophistication of the measurements that researchers have constructed. The claims that Stevens made are controversial, and some psychologists believe that many are overstated, and mathematical statisticians do not agree with or follow the suggestion that Stevens made. On the other hand, many psychologists still take some of the ideas Stevens proposed quite seriously

According to Stevens, there are four different scales of measurement that vary in sophistication. Of these four, some do not lend themselves to very much in the way of statistical analysis, whereas others permit sophisticated and complex statistical treatment.

Nominal Scales

The simplest form of measurement involves the **nominal scale** of measurement. This scale is generally limited to counting the frequency with which observed cases fall into certain categories. So in psychological research on preferences, people may be given a number of choices from which to select what they like best. At the end, the investigator will be able to count the number of people who prefer each of the choices.

The data are frequencies of occurrence in categories. The only real statistical analysis appropriate for this type of data involves examination as to whether there are more or fewer occurrences in a given category compared to expectations. Furthermore, any numbers associated with the data are not meaningful. For instance, if people are categorized as female or male, females may be put in a category numbered as 1 and males in a category numbered as 2. These numbers do not have any mathematical or statistical meaning and could be represented by numbers or any other arbitrary designation.

Ordinal Scales

A slightly more sophisticated form of measurement involves differentiating observations on the basis of relative magnitude or position, which is what occurs with **ordinal scales**. So, for example, if people are ranked in order of attractiveness, the most attractive person (given a rank of 1) has a lower number than the second most attractive person (given a rank of 2) and so on.

We can develop relative ranks, but we do not know if the difference in attractiveness of people ranked 1 and 2 is the same as the difference in attractiveness of people ranked 19 and 20. In both instances, the two people being compared are one rank apart, but it could be the case that people ranked 1 through 19 are all just about the same in attractiveness, but the person ranked 20 is quite a bit less attractive.

In a real example, if you look at the rankings of number of career home runs hit by major league baseball players in North America, you will see that positions 1 and 2 differ by 7 home runs (762 to 755), whereas positions 301 and 302 differ by one (198 to 197). These data illustrate that with a scale that uses rank ordering, we can say that one observation is more or less than another on the dimension of interest to us, but we cannot ascertain how much different. We can just order them.

Interval Scales

Interval scales involve a continuum of values whose differences matter in a meaningful way. That is, if one pair of numbers differs by a specific amount (e.g., by 5 units) and another pair of numbers differs by that same amount, the actual magnitude of the difference is the same for both pairs, unlike the situation with ranks on an ordinal scale, where differences in ranks do not always represent the same amount of change (as noted in the example about home runs above).

A common example of an interval scale involves temperature measured in Fahrenheit or Celsius. The physical difference between 5 and 10 degrees is the same as the difference between 85 and 90 degrees. (The psychological difference may be quite different, however.)

The value of numbers on an interval scale is that they can be manipulated arithmetically in a meaningful way. As such, when data are represented on an interval scale, researchers can use sophisticated statistical tests to help them answer questions about behavior. Data on nominal and ordinal scales typically do not lend themselves to complicated statistics.

Ratio Scales

The most sophisticated kind of measurement occurs on a **ratio scale**, which has an absolute zero value below which no scores are possible. An example would be the number of coins in your pocket. It can be zero or some number greater than zero. An additional property of scores on a ratio scale is that you can talk about ratios (hence the name of the scale). That is, if you have 10 coins in your pocket and a friend has 5 coins, you have twice as many as he does. Such ratios are not appropriate for scores on any of the other scales.

In psychology, measurements on a ratio scale might include the time it takes to complete a task or the number of trials it takes to learn a task. Most of our measurements are not on ratio scales, however. For instance, if you are measuring intelligence, you may use a test of some kind. It would be possible for somebody to get a score of zero, but it is not likely that the person actually has no intelligence. You just have not measured the intelligence particularly well in that case.

In reality, in psychological research the scale of measurement can be deceptive. Using intelligence test scores as an example again, it would not make sense to say that a person with an intelligence test score of 80 has twice as much intelligence as a person with a score of 40. Another way of looking at the issue is to consider what happens when you measure levels of extraversion; if one person scores 20 on a given inventory and another scores 10, it does not indicate that the first person is twice as extraverted because increases in the numerical scores may not reflect consistent and orderly increases in the extraversion. We may only know that a higher score is associated with more extraversion.

Finally, if you are measuring learning by the number of items correctly answered on a test, a score of 50 correct is twice as many as a score of 25. This measurement legitimately involves a ratio scale. On the other hand, it may not be the case that the person with the higher score knows twice as much as a person with a score of 25. In discussing amount of knowledge, we might be able to say only that one person probably knows more than another, which involves an ordinal scale.

As noted above, some psychological researchers regard scales of measurement as very important in the determination of the statistical analyses they employ. Other psychologists think that the issue is largely irrelevant. Nonetheless, the issue of scales of measurement is a regular topic of discussion as researchers debate the validity of statistical approaches to research.

WHY PSYCHOLOGISTS USE STATISTICS

When researchers conduct studies, they usually end up with a data set that requires some analysis. This is where statistics enters into the picture. For example, if a research study involves 100 participants and each of these responds to multiple stimuli, there is a lot of information to sift through, categorize, summarize, and/or interpret. Each of these tasks makes use of statistics.

In one study, psychologist Bernard Beins and colleague Shawn O'Toole examined the relation between sense of humor and personality characteristics among 109 people. Each participant responded to a 24-item sense of humor inventory, to four different personality inventories that included a total of 50 items, and to two questions about their perceptions of their own sense of humor. So each person provided 76 data points. Consequently, across all participants, there were over 8,000 separate data points.

It would be overwhelming to try and make sense out of such a large pool of data just by looking at the numbers. And there are other studies that include a larger number of participants and more data from each one. In fact, in a follow-up study, Beins and his colleagues tested 202 participants, each of whom contributed 132 data points, for a total of 26,664 numbers in the data set.

The strategy in dealing with such large amounts of data is to use statistics that summarize the data in an easy and convenient manner. This approach involves **descriptive statistics**, which reduce a potentially large data set to a few numbers that convey useful information about the data.

An additional use of statistics involves assessing the reliability of the results. That is, if the researchers were to repeat a study, how likely would it be that the results would be similar the second time? When the statistical tests indicate that a **replication** (i.e., a repetition) of the study would lead to a similar outcome, investigators say that the findings are **statistically significant**. Researchers use **inferential statistics** to help draw conclusions (i.e., inferences) about the reliability of their data.

The terminology here can be confusing. When researchers say that their results are significant, the investigators mean that the results would be likely to recur in a replication of the study. It does not mean that the findings are *significant* in the everyday use of the word. So, for example, with the large number of students taking the SAT each year, an increase of two points in the average score from one year to the next would be statistically significant. But such a small change would not be all that important. The term *significance* in statistics relates to reliability, not importance.

The reason for this unusual use of the word *significance* was that the first statisticians used this word to mean that something *signified* something; that is, "significant difference" told us something meaningful (but not that the difference itself was meaningful).

Descriptive Statistics

The two types of descriptive statistics that researchers use are measures of **central tendency** and measures of **variability**. These measurements give us important information about general tendencies in a data set, such as what is a typical score and how much spread exists in the data.

Measures of Central Tendency

Psychologists are likely to use three measures of central tendency (although there are more than three). These measures are types of averages or typical scores. The most common measure of central tendency is the **arithmetic mean**, which is what most people would simply call the **average** in everyday language. Very often, researchers refer to this value simply as the **mean**.

A second measure of central tendency is the **median**. This is the middle value that you get if you list scores from low to high and identify the score in the middle of the list. The median is particularly useful when scores are bounded in one direction but not in the other. For instance, the time to respond to a stimulus cannot be less than zero, but there could be very high values at the other end of the list. The third measure of central tendency is the **mode**, which is simply the most frequent score in a distribution.

Measures of Variability

Sometimes it is useful to know not only what constitutes a typical score in a distribution of numbers, but also how much the scores are spread apart, that is, their variability. If a teacher administered a test to a class and the scores of most students were quite similar, it would say one thing; if some students had very low scores while other students had very high scores, it would say something else.

The most common measure of variability is the **standard deviation**, which is itself a kind of average because standard deviation tells us the average difference between the mean and other scores in the data set. That is, if the mean of a distribution of numbers were 50 and the standard deviation were 10, those numbers would tell us that we could expect many scores to be within 10 points of the mean. In this example, it would mean that a lot of the scores would be between 40 and 60.

Another common measure of variability is the **range**, which is the distance from the smallest value to the largest. It is an easy value to compute, but it may

Computing Descriptive Statistics

Random sample of 10 responses to the question, "How good is your sense of humor" on a scale of 1 (*not good*) to 10 (*very good*), from the research example by Beins and O'Toole.

10 7 8 7 3 6 8 8 8 5

Computing the Mean: Add all the numbers and divide by the number of data points.

The sum of the ten numbers is 70. Dividing 70 by 10 gives us a mean of 7.0. (In most distributions, the mean usually involves values that are not whole numbers.)

Computing the Median: List the scores from lowest to highest and find the middle score.

The scores in order are 3, 5, 6, 7, 7, 8, 8, 8, 8, 10. With an even number of scores, there is no score exactly in the middle, so we take the average of scores in the fifth and sixth position, the two middle-most numbers. In this case, the median is 7.5.

Computing the Mode: Find the most frequently occurring score. In this set of numbers, it is 8.

Computing the standard deviation: This statistic sounds complicated, but it is not all that difficult if you take it step by step.

Subtract the mean from each score in the distribution and square the result; then add the squares. Because there are 10 numbers in the data set, there will be 10 differences to square:

$(10-7)^2 + (7-7)^2 + (8-7)^2 + (7-7)^2 + (4-7)^2 + (6-7)^2 + (8-7)^2 + (8-7)^2 +$
$(8-7)^2 + (5-7)^2 = 9 + 0 + 1 + 0 + 9 + 1 + 1 + 1 + 1 + 4 = 27$

If you divide the sum by the number of data points, you get 27/10 - 2.7.

Finally, take the square root of the division. The square root of 2.7 is 1.64, which is the standard deviation. (There are two different formulas for the standard deviation that researchers use depending on the details of the data analysis. The other formula involves dividing by the number of data points minus one. In this case, the division would be 27/9 = 3, so the square root would be 1.73.)

Computing the range: Find the difference between the smallest and the largest values. In this example, the range of scores is from 3 to 10, which equals 7.

William Sealy Gossett, inventor of the t test in 1908. *(Wikipedia)*

not be very useful because a single extreme score will increase the value of the range so that it does not give a very good depiction of how far most scores are spread.

As with the measures of central tendency, there are other measures of variability than the ones mentioned in this section. But because they are rarely used in psychology, we will not pursue them here.

Inferential Statistics

The final statistics to be discussed here are the inferential statistics that psychologists use to test the reliability of their findings. These statistics can get quite complicated, but the logic is reasonably simple. When researchers want to find out if two groups differ in their average scores, they use inferential statistics to assess whether the difference is large enough to be considered real or suffi-

Testing for a Significant Difference

The data discussed here come from the humor research by Beins and O'Toole in which the data on self-ratings of sense of humor by men and by women can be compared. We can use the *t* test to answer the question of whether men and women differ in their self-reported sense of humor on a scale of 1 (*not good*) to 10 (*very good*).

Our question is whether the difference between men and women is big enough for us to believe that they systematically differ in the way they report their sense of humor. The other possibility is that the difference between men and women occurred for unpredictable or unknown reasons unrelated to gender.

$$M_{men} = 7.6$$
$$M_{women} = 8.0$$

The relevant test here is the *t* test. The calculations are not difficult, but there are quite a few steps to go through to compute the value of the *t* test by hand, so only the conclusion will appear here. (Generally, researchers use computerized statistical analyses rather than hand calculations because of the many steps required for hand calculations.) It turns out that this value of *t* is significant, so based on this sample, we would conclude that men and women reliably differ in their estimations of how good their sense of humor is. The self-rating by men is higher than that of women.

Further analysis of data reveals that men and women do not differ significantly in their overall sense of humor according to an inventory that measures sense of humor. Women just rate themselves lower than men do. On the other hand, men actually do have a higher productive sense of humor (e.g., telling jokes) than women do. The standard statistical tests have generated some controversy. Many researchers believe that data analysis that relies on them alone is insufficient. Nonetheless, inferential statistics are still nearly universal in data analysis in psychology.

ciently small that it is probably accidental. If you remember that logic, it is easy to understand the point of inferential statistics.

One of the oldest tests of differences between groups is the **Student's t test**, usually just called the *t* test. It was invented by William Gossett in 1908 as a test for significant differences between means of small groups.

Two other statisticians who had an enormous impact on the generation of inferential statistics are Ronald Aylmer Fisher who developed the analysis of variance (and for whom the *F* statistic is named) and Karl Pearson who was instrumental in creation of correlational analysis. Fisher and Pearson were bitter rivals who seem to have had only one friend in common, William Gossett.

Further Reading

Best, Joel. *Damned Lies and Statistics: Untangling Numbers from the Media, Politicians, and Activists.* Berkeley, CA, US: University of California Press, 2001.

Huff, Darrell. *How to Lie with Statistics.* New York, NY, US: W. W. Norton, 1954.

Paulos, John A. *Once upon a Number.* New York, NY, US. Basic Books, 1998.

GLOSSARY

acquiescence A bias in which a respondent is likely to say "yes" to questions, regardless of content, or to answer in apparent agreement to a surveyor's belief.

active deception The process of keeping participants from knowing the true purpose of a study by giving them false information about the purpose of the study.

archival research A research methodology in which existing information, such as public records, newspaper stories, etc., provide data for drawing conclusions about behaviors.

biosocial effects Biological effects (like sex) of the researcher on a participant's behavior.

California Personality Inventory (CPI) A personality inventory using some questions from the MMPI; it is less oriented toward psychological problems than the MMPI and more oriented toward everyday personality issues.

case studies A research methodology in which a single person is studied in great depth, often with no manipulation of independent variables.

central tendency Measures of what constitutes a typical or average score in a data set.

closed-ended question An item on a questionnaire that has responses generated by the researcher from which a respondent chooses an answer; common examples are true/false and multiple choice questions.

coefficient alpha A reliability statistic that computes an average reliability value based on all possible split-half reliabilities.

compensatory follow-up   The process of contacting participants after potentially risky studies to see if there are any long-term negative consequences.

concurrent validity   A type of validity associated with whether a test score is reliably associated with another, related measurement at the time the test is taken.

confound   An unwanted factor that affects the behavior of participants in one group of an experiment but not other groups, obscuring the effects of an independent variable on the dependent variable.

construct validity   A type of validity associated with the degree to which a test adequately measures an abstract hypothetical construct.

content validity   A type of validity associated with whether the content of a test is appropriate for what the test is intended to measure; this type of validity is relevant for tests of knowledge or skill.

control   A goal of scientific research related to the ability to use explanation of the causes of a behavior to control that behavior.

control group   A group in an experiment that receives no treatment and is simply measured with respect to the dependent variable.

convenience sampling   A nonprobability approach to sampling in which researchers use participant groups that are available and convenient.

correlation coefficient   A statistical value that reflects the strength of association between two variables.

correlational design   A research design in which investigators measure participants' responses without manipulating variables in order to see if two or more variables change together in predictable ways.

correlational research   A research methodology characterized by measurement of multiple variables to see if there is a predictable relation between the value on one variable and the value on another.

covariance rule   Principle of determining causation relating to an effect occurring reliably in the presence of a causal factor.

cover story   A story concocted by a researcher to disguise the true purpose of a study so that participants do not alter their behaviors to conform to what they perceive as expectations.

criterion-related validity   A type of validity associated with whether a predictor variable predicts a specific behavior, or criterion.

culture-fair test   A concept relating to creation of intelligence tests that are not biased either in favor of or against people of differing cultural backgrounds.

culture-free test   A concept relating to creation of intelligence tests that are completely free of reliance on knowledge or ability associated with cultural backgrounds of people who take the test; psychologists generally regard this as an impossible attainment.

curvilinear relation   A relation between variables; change of a certain magnitude on one variable is associated with variable amounts of change on the second variable, depending on where on a number line the first variable falls.

data-driven conclusion   A characteristic of scientific research associated with the use of data from research to draw conclusions about behavior, thought, and emotion.

debriefing   Informing participants after a study about the nature of the study and any deception that was involved.

dehoaxing   Informing participants after a study about the nature of any deception involved in the research.

demand characteristic   The tendency of participants to act in certain ways because they think that a researcher wants or expects them to.

dependent variable   A variable whose value may change (or be dependent on) the value of an independent variable.

description   A goal of scientific research related to documenting the existence of psychological phenomena.

descriptive statistics   Statistics that summarize a data set, providing information on what constitutes an average or typical value in the set and the degree of spread across scores.

desensitization   The process of counteracting any potentially negative effects that participants may experience as a result of taking part in a study.

directionality   A problem in determining causation, specifically if there are two variables that vary together reliably and it is not possible to identify which is the cause and which is the effect.

Dissociative Experiences Scale   A 28-scale inventory designed to assess the degree to which people integrate their emotions, thoughts, and behaviors in everyday life.

double-blind study   A research study in which neither participants nor researchers know the treatment or control group to which a participant has been assigned.

ecological fallacy   The problem of assuming that measurements that hold true for a group as a whole are good predictors of behaviors of an individual within that group.

emic   A research finding that scientists believe holds true within a single culture and that is culturally bound and not generalizable to people in other cultures.

etic   A research finding that scientists believe hold true across cultures and is not dependent on cultural context.

experiment   A research methodology characterized by manipulation and control of independent variables to see the effect on behavior as measured through dependent variables.

explanation   A goal of scientific research related to identifying the causes of behaviors.

extraneous variable   A variable unknown to or undesired by a researcher that, along with an independent variable, affects the value of a dependent variable

Hawthorne effect   Changes in participants' behaviors caused by knowing they are being observed by the researcher.

hypothetical construct   A concept that is not directly observable but that a psychologist believes is helpful in understanding human behavior.

impression management   A bias in which a respondent intentionally answers questions in order to make a good impression on the researcher.

independent variable   A variable that a researcher manipulates in an experiment in order to see the effect of a change in its value on some subsequent behavior.

inferential statistics   Statistics that provide information about whether a researcher can be confident that the results would be reliable across different studies.

institutional review board (IRB)   A group of people who review research proposals to make sure that the project is not likely to result in harm to participants.

internal validity   Principle of determining causation relating to the idea that one has confidence in identifying a causal factor only after being able to rule out other potential causal factors.

interval scale   A measurement scale on which it is possible to identify measurement values in terms of absolute differences between scores; interval scales are often seen as permitting the use of sophisticated statistical analysis.

Kaufman Brief Intelligence Test (K-BIT)   A commonly used test of intelligence based on concepts of fluid and crystallized intelligence.

Likert-type scale   A self-report measurement scale, usually with scores from 1 to some number (e.g., 1 to 7) on which a research participant assigns a value (e.g., *On a scale of 1 to 7, how energetic do you feel?*)

linear correlation   A relation between variables; specifically when a change of a certain magnitude on one variable is associated with a fixed amount of change on a second variable, no matter where on a number line those variables fall.

longitudinal research A research methodology in which an investigator studies a group of people over an extended period of time, ranging from fairly short periods like days or weeks to years or even decades.

mean A measure of central tendency that identifies what is referred to as the average in everyday language.

median The middle-most score in a data set when the numbers are ordered from lowest to highest.

Minnesota Multiphasic Personality Inventory (MMPI) A personality inventory consisting of objectively scored items designed to provide information on ten psychological dimensions; it is one of the most widely used tests in mental health screening.

mode The measure of central tendency representing the most frequently occurring score in a data set; there may be multiple modes.

Multidimensional Aptitude Battery (MAB) A test of aptitude consisting of 10 verbal and performance scales.

multiple regression A statistical approach in which the values of two or more variables are used to predict the value of another variable.

Myers-Briggs Type Inventory (MBTI) A psychological test based on Carl Jung's theory and designed to identify basic ways in which a person perceives and responds to events in life.

nominal scale A measurement scale in which observations are assigned to categories (e.g., female and male); no arithmetic operations are appropriate on this scale other than counting the number of occurrences assigned to categories.

nonlinear relation A relation between two variables in which a change in the value of one variable has an effect of changing magnitude, depending on the position of the first variable on a number line.

nonprobability sampling An approach to sampling that not always lead to samples that are representative of a known population.

objectivity A characteristic of scientific research associated with well-defined definitions of behaviors and variables that psychologists measure.

observational research A research methodology characterized by recording of naturally occurring behaviors, generally without manipulation of variables or intervention by the researcher.

open-ended question An item on a questionnaire to which respondents provide their own responses rather than using alternatives presented by the researcher.

operational definition   The means by which an abstract, not directly measurable hypothetical construct is measured in a research project; the construct is defined in terms of how it is measured.

optimizing   The response tendency to search for the best possible answer to a survey question.

ordinal scale   A measurement scale on which values signify ordinal values; it is possible to identify that observations are bigger, faster, higher, and so forth, but not to assess their absolute differences.

passive deception   The process of keeping participants from knowing the true purpose of a study by failing to provide them with relevant information.

placebo group   A group in an experiment that receives an inactive treatment so participants believe that they are receiving an active treatment.

prediction   A goal of scientific research related to identifying the conditions that lead to behaviors of interest to investigators.

predictive validity   A type of validity associated with whether a test score reliably predicts a criterion measure.

probability sampling   The practice of creating a sample from a population so that each member of the population has a certain, known probability of being selected.

projective tests   A class of psychological tests that consist of ambiguous or incomplete stimuli, like pictures, images, or sentences, to which a person responds.

psychometrics   An area of quantitative psychology that deals with assessment of reliability and validity characteristics of tests.

psychophysics   An area of psychology that studies the relation between physical stimuli and people's psychological responses to them.

psychosocial effects   Effects of a researcher's personal characteristics like personality on responses of a participant.

public research   A characteristic of science related to researchers' willingness to make their data and research findings public so others can evaluate them; this usually takes the form of publications in scientific books or journals and presentations at scientific conferences.

random assignment   Placing participants in research groups according to some random process.

ratio scale   A measurement scale on which it is possible to identify ratios between scores as well as absolute differences; scores on a ratio scale have a zero value that constitutes the smallest possible score, negative numbers not being possible.

regression analysis   A statistical approach in which the value of one variable is used to predict the value of a second variable.

reliability   A property of tests that deals with the extent to which a person's scores are consistent across different items on the test, with repeated testing, or on alternate forms of the test.

replication   Repeating research to see if the results of a second study are similar to those of the original study.

response bias   Consistent response tendencies by participants in answering questions, which do not represent their actual attitudes, memories, or thoughts.

Rorschach test   A projective test consisting of 10 ambiguous visual stimuli designed to generate responses that provide information about unconscious processes.

sampling frame   The pool of possible survey respondents from which a researcher selects participants.

satisficing   The response tendency to produce the first acceptable answer to a survey question, even if it is not the best answer.

self-deception positivity   A bias in which participants unknowingly answer questions in a way that portray them positively, reflecting beliefs about themselves that are not accurate.

simple random sampling   An approach to sampling in which each person typically has the same chance of being selected.

single-blind study   A research study in which participants do not know to which treatment or control group they have been assigned. Technically, it also refers to the researcher (rather than the participant) not knowing which group he or she is dealing with, but this type of single blinding would be rare.

social desirability bias   A bias in which a respondent either knowingly or unintentionally answers questions in a certain way for the sole purpose of looking good in the eyes of the researcher.

split-half reliability   A form of reliability that deals with the comparability of a person's scores when a test is split into two subtests and the scores compared.

standard deviation   The measure of variability that indicates the average amount by which a typical score in a data set will deviate from the mean.

Stanford-Binet Intelligence Scales (SB5)   A commonly used test of intelligence, originally based on a test developed by Alfred Binet and Théodore Simon in the early 20th century.

statistical significance   When researchers conclude that research results are reliable, that is, that they would be consistent if the research were to be repeated; in this use, *significance* implies reliability, not necessarily that the results are important.

stratified random sampling   The approach to sampling in which the population is subdivided into categories, such as female and male, from which random sampling is then conducted.

student's *t* test   A commonly used statistical test designed to assess whether the difference between two means is great enough to be considered statistically significant.

survey research   A research methodology characterized by questioning respondents on issues of thought, attitude, and behavior; answers can be based on a selection of alternatives given by the researcher in response to a question or on nondirected answers generated by the respondent.

synesthesia   A phenomenon in which a person receives sensory stimulation in one modality (e.g., audition) that is experienced in another modality, such as hearing a sound that is consistently experienced visually.

telescoping   A memory phenomenon in which respondents believe that events have occurred more recently than they actually have, named for the effect of looking through a telescope so that distant objects appear close.

temporal precedence rule   Principle of determining causation relating to the fact that the causal variable has to precede the effect.

test bias   A potential problem of tests that discriminate for or against people from certain groups; a number of widely used, standardized tests are free from statistical bias.

test-retest reliability   A form of reliability that deals with the degree to which a person's score on a test is consistent in repeated testing.

Thematic Apperception test   A projective test consisting of a set of ambiguous pictures about which a person creates a story designed to reflect unconscious motivation.

third-variable problem   A problem in determining causation in cases when neither of two variables that vary together may cause variation in the other; rather, there may be a third variable that is affecting them both.

validity   The extent to which a measurement actually measures what it is intended to.

variability   The degree to which scores in a data set are clustered or spread apart.

variable   Anything that is measurable and can take on more than one value.

verifiability   A characteristic of science related to the ability of researchers to test previous research findings to see if the findings can be repeated.

Wechsler Adult Intelligence Scale (WAIS)   A commonly used test of intelligence, developed by David Wechsler; the test includes both verbal and nonverbal components.

BIBLIOGRAPHY

Ambrose, Nicoline Grinager, and Ehud Yairi. "The Tudor Study: Data and Ethics." *American Journal of Speech-Language Pathology* 11, no. 2 (2002):190–203.

American Psychological Association, Washington, D.C. "Ethical principles of psychologists and code of conduct." *American Psychologist* 57, no. 12 (2002): 1060–1073.

Ayduk, Özlem, Anett Gyurak, and Anna Luerssen. "Individual differences in the rejection-aggression link in the hot sauce paradigm: The case of rejection sensitivity." *Journal of Experimental Social Psychology* 44, no. 3 (2008): 775–782.

Beins, Bernard C. *Research Methods: A Tool for Life*, 2nd ed. Boston: Allyn & Bacon, 2009.

Beins, Bernard C., and Shawn M. O'Toole. "Searching for the sense of humor: Stereotypes of ourselves and others." *Europe's Journal of Psychology,* 6 (2010): 267–287. Available at http://www.ejop.org/archives/2010/08/index.html.

Best, Joel. *Damned Lies and Statistics: Untangling Numbers from the Media, Politicians, and Activists*. Berkeley, Calif.: University of California Press, 2001.

———. *Stat-Spotting: A Field Guide to Identifying Dubious Data*. Berkeley, Calif.: University of California Press, 2008.

Blass, Thomas. "From New Haven to Santa Clara: A historical perspective on the Milgram Obedience Experiments." *American Psychologist* 64, no. 1 (2009): 37–45.

Burger, Jerry M. "Replicating Milgram: Would people still obey today?" *American Psychologist* 64, no. 1 (2009): 1–11.

Bushman, Brad J., and Craig A. Anderson. "Media violence and the American public: Scientific facts versus media misinformation." *American Psychologist* 56, no. 6–7 (2001): 477–489.

Buss, Arnold H., and Mark Perry. "The aggression questionnaire." *Journal of Personality and Social Psychology* 63, no. 3 (1992): 452–459.

Cytowic, Richard E. *The Man Who Tasted Shapes: A Bizarre Medical Mystery Offers Revolutionary Insights into Emotions, Reasoning, and Consciousness.* New York: G. P. Putnam & Sons.

Davis, Stephen F. (Ed.). *Handbook of Research Methods in Experimental Psychology.* Boston: Blackwell, 2005.

Dr. Thomas Blass presents StanleyMilgram.com. Accessed at http://www.stanleymilgram.com/.

Ethical Principles of Psychologists and Code of Conduct with the 2010 Amendments. 2010. http://www.apa.org/ethics/code/index.aspx.

Gardner, Howard. E. *Multiple Intelligences.* New York: Basic Books, 2006.

Gould, Stephen. J. *The Mismeasure of Man.* New York: W.W. Norton, 1996.

Gregory, R.J. *Psychological Testing: History, Principles, and Applications.* Boston: Allyn & Bacon, 2004.

Gruenewald, Paul J., Fred W. Johnson, William R. Ponicki, and Elizabeth A. LaScala. "A dose response perspective on college drinking and related problems." *Addiction* 105, no. 2 (2010): 257–269.

Huff, Darrell. *How to Lie with Statistics.* New York: Norton, 1982.

Joseph, Stephen, P. Alex Linley, Jake Harwood, Christopher Alan Lewis, and Patrick McCollam. "Rapid assessment of well-being: The short depression-happiness scale (SDHS)." *Psychology and Psychotherapy: Theory, Research and Practice* 77, no. 4 (2004): 463–478.

Krosnick, Jon A. "Survey research." *Annual Review of Psychology* 50 (1999): 537–567.

Lieberman, Joel D., Sheldon Solomon, Jeff Greenberg, and Holly A. McGregor. "A hot new way to measure aggression: Hot sauce allocation." *Aggressive Behavior* 25, no. 5 (1999): 331–348.

Lifton, Robert Jay. *The Nazi Doctors.* New York: Basic Books, 1999.

MacLeod, Colin, and Lynlee Campbell. "Memory accessibility and probability judgments: An experimental evaluation of the availability heuristic." *Journal of Personality and Social Psychology* 63, no. 6 (1992): 890–902.

Meltzoff, Julian. "Ethics in research." *Journal of Aggression, Maltreatment & Trauma* 11, no. 3 (2005): 311–336.

Pashler, Harold, Mark McDaniel, Doug Rohrer, and Robert Bjork. "Learning styles: Concepts and evidence." *Psychological Science in the Public Interest* 9, no. 3 (2008): 105–119.

Pettigrew, Thomas F. *How to Think Like a Social Scientist*. New York: Harper-Collins, 1996.

Phillips, John L. *How to Think About Statistics*. New York: Freeman, 1988.

Ritter, Dominik, and Mike Eslea. "Hot sauce, toy guns, and graffiti: A critical account of current laboratory aggression paradigms." *Aggressive Behavior* 31, no. 3 (2005): 407–419.

Rosenthal, R. and Ralph R. Rosnow. *The Volunteer Subject*. New York: Wiley. 1975.

Rosnow, Ralph R, and Robert Rosenthal. *People Studying People: Artifacts and Ethics in Behavioral Research*. New York: Freeman, 1997.

Sales, Bruce D. and Susan Folkman. *Ethics in Research with Human Participants*. Washington, D.C.: American Psychological Association, 2000.

Salsburg, David. *The Lady Tasting Tea: How Statistics Revolutionized Statistics in the Twentieth Century*. New York: Freeman, 2001.

Stanovich, Keith E. *How to Think Straight About Psychology*, 9th ed. Boston: Allyn & Bacon, 2009.

Steenkamp, Jan-Benedict E. M., Martijn G. De Jong, and Hans Baumgartner. Socially desirable response tendencies in survey research. *Journal of Marketing Research* 47, no. 4 (2010): 199–214.

Sternberg, Robert. J. *Beyond IQ: A Triarchic Theory of Human Intelligence*. New York: Cambridge University Press, 1984.

———. *Wisdom, Intelligence, and Creativity Synthesized*. New York: Cambridge University Press, 2007.

Takahashi, Hidehiko, Masato Matsuura, Michihiko Koeda, Noriaki Yahata, Tetsuya Suhara, Motoichiro Kato, and Yoshiro Okubo. "Brain activations during judgments of positive self-conscious emotion and positive basic emotion: Pride and joy." *Cerebral Cortex* 18, no. 4) (2008): 898–903.

Wimer, David J., and Bernard C. Beins. "Expectations and perceived humor." *Humor: International Journal of Humor Research* 21, no. 3 (2008): 347–363.

INDEX

Index note: Page numbers followed by *g* indicate glossary entries.